THE SUZY LAMPLUGH STORY

Andrew Stephen was formerly Senior Editor on *The Sunday Times Magazine*, and now writes for *The Observer*. He was based in Northern Ireland for three years and has reported from many parts of the world. In 1984 he was Feature Writer of the Year in the British Press Awards. He is married and lives in London.

The
Suzy Lamplugh
Story

ANDREW STEPHEN

faber and faber

LONDON · BOSTON

First published in 1988
by Faber and Faber Limited
3 Queen Square London WCIN 3AU

Phototypeset by Input Typesetting, Ltd, London
Printed in Great Britain by
Richard Clay Ltd, Bungay, Suffolk
All rights reserved

British Library Cataloguing in Publication Data

Stephen, Andrew
The Suzy Lamplugh Story.
1. Missing persons – England –
London
I. Title
001.9′4 HV6762.G7
ISBN 0–571–15152–3
ISBN 0–571–15415–8 Pbk

List of Illustrations

Chapter One

It was a peculiarly English affair: a damp spring morning, an Anglican church south of London, choirboys and girls in red cassocks and white ruffs. The vicar spoke of 'the mystery of the suffering'. A large congregation hammered out 'Dear Lord and Father of Mankind', 'Guide me, O Thou Great Redeemer' and 'Love Divine, All Loves Excelling'.

But then Paul Lamplugh, a fifty-five-year-old solicitor, went quietly to the front of the church and in just twelve seconds said why this was also a unique occasion. 'While we do not believe that Suzy is alive,' he told the hushed congregation, 'we also do not believe that she is dead. *That is the paradox.*'

Seven months before, at 12.40 one Monday lunchtime, his daughter Susannah Jane Lamplugh, aged twenty-five, had left the estate agent's office in London where she worked – apparently to meet a client called 'Mr Kipper', and then to show him a house. Her car, with her purse and straw hat untouched inside, was discovered later that evening. But no trace of Susannah was found. Nor was there any hint of a struggle, or any witness who saw anything remotely untoward on a summer afternoon in a busy area of London. No client called 'Mr Kipper' ever came forward.

Within days the name of Susannah Lamplugh was familiar across the country, for the response to the mystery was quite unprecedented. To the media she quickly became 'Suzy', the archetypal, wholesome and beautiful girl-next-door, everyone's daughter, sister, friend. Her mother Diana soon had instant fame too, and before long was rarely out of the limelight.

But of Susannah there was no trace at all, not the slightest clue as to how or why she had disappeared.

So although she was absent this March morning, the service was not a funeral, and instead of mourning clothes her friends and relatives wore the light colours and buttonhole flowers more usually seen at a wedding or christening. Her mother had chosen a daffodil-yellow silk dress and black hat for the occasion. There were smiles instead of tears, laughter instead of weeping. The Order of Service called it an 'Act of Healing in Celebration of the Life' of Susannah Lamplugh – 'a life', said the vicar, 'in which until her abduction there was much to celebrate'. And, although some in the church had mixed feelings about it, there was also the dedication of an organization set up by her mother, called The Suzy Lamplugh Trust.

It was all another extraordinary paradox: that an ordinary, unremarkable life had in retrospect become so celebrated. The family of Susannah Lamplugh had never led such interesting, stimulating, even powerful lives before her disappearance. But now her mother – who just a year before had been a suburban swimming teacher and co-founder of 'Slimnastics' – could pick up the phone and ask to speak to the Home Secretary, or entertain unseen millions on live television talk shows or be in demand for lectures up and down the country. She had become an intriguing media personality, and enjoyed it too. 'Now we are probably (bar the Royals) one of the most well-known families in Britain,' she had written in a family letter. But with such fulfilment had also come sorrow, torment and terrible guilt.

Famous people, none of whom had actually known Susannah, had joined the congregation. The Reverend Dr Colin Morris, a distinguished broadcaster, former President of the Methodist Conference and future Controller of the BBC in Northern Ireland, gave an address: 'How many lives can you touch when you are twenty-five, a happy south London girl?' he asked the congregation. 'And yet Suzy has touched and is touching the lives of a growing number of people. Why do I, why do I call her Suzy naturally? *I never met her. I never set eyes on her. I knew nothing of her until I met the Lamplughs.* Why do I call her Suzy? *Because she's touched my life and you are here because she's touched your life too.*' Richard Briers, a popular television comedy actor, joined in with a reading.

Police, journalists, mediums, broadcasters, clairvoyants: all were there too, all come to pay their respects to someone who had never known such attention in her life. They were scattered among Susannah's close family, relatives, friends, her former headmistresses, estate agent colleagues, boyfriends, even the odd amateur sleuth who with the assorted mediums and clairvoyants had made it their business to solve the mystery of Susannah's disappearance.

But had Susannah been abducted as the vicar had suggested? There were absolutely no clues to confirm that she had been – but equally certainly, none to suggest that she had gone off of her own volition either. This had not stopped ideas, theories, even accusations, ricocheting round this diverse group now gathered in All Saints Church, East Sheen. Some at the service even believed the man responsible for her disappearance – if, indeed, such a man existed – was there in the church among them that morning. Diana Lamplugh referred to them as 'suspects': men who for one reason or another were close to Susannah, and who had been unable to give entirely satisfactory accounts of their movements on the day she went missing. A clairvoyant, convinced she beyond others had some inner communication with the truth, even went up to one former boyfriend of Susannah in the church and told him: 'You're the one. I *know* you did it.'

Joining discreetly in the service, meanwhile, were three men who actually knew more about the case than anyone else present – Detective Inspector Peter Johnstone and Detective Sergeant Michael Barley of the Metropolitan Police, and the man who was their senior until he had retired two months before, Detective Superintendent Nicholas Carter. Between them they had examined every possibility, considered every angle, spent countless days and nights mulling over what on earth could have happened to Susannah. Teams of policemen and women under their command had compiled 26,000 separate index cards, each with information on Susannah, her life, and on people police thought might be able to shed light on what had happened to her.

For the detectives, the routine police file opened on the evening she did not return – file FF584/1/54 – had developed into the biggest and most involved missing person inquiry in history. It had also become the most touching and exasperating case of their careers. In many ways they now knew more about Susannah, her life, her habits, her friends and her lovers, than even her family in the front pews knew, or the amateur sleuths or mediums or journalists or all-knowing clairvoyants.

They had quickly discovered from their investigations that Susannah kept much of her life to herself: friends and contacts whom her family never knew about, boyfriends and lovers equally unknown to the 'Putney Set' (the label given by the Lamplughs and others to a close-knit group of middle-class professionals with whom she often mixed), a private life of some complexity of which no one person was fully apprised. The media picture of Suzy Lamplugh did not tell the whole story. Indeed, to many acquaintances she was not even known

4

as 'Suzy'. On the liner *QE*2 – where she had worked as a beautician, and from which she had seen the world and formulated a dream to settle in South Africa with a boyfriend from the ship – her nickname was 'H', because she told colleagues firmly that her name was 'Susannah – with an H'. Relatives and friends tended to call her simply 'Suze'.

Few if any innocent lives had thus ever come under such relentless scrutiny. But as the quintessentially English sounds of an Anglican church service died away, one inescapable and sad fact remained unchanged: that Susannah Jane Lamplugh, the popular, hard-working and ambitious young woman who was the focus for the service, was palpably absent. Hardly any of the people pouring out of the church into the gentle sunlight outside ever expected to see her again. Two hundred and sixteen days after she failed to return to her office that routine Monday lunchtime, her disappearance was as much a mystery as ever.

Chapter Two

The phone call came, as such calls always do, when it was least expected. It was just before five o'clock in the afternoon on the first day of Diana Lamplugh's summer holidays – 28 July 1986 – and she was sitting on the floor in her husband's study going through some paperwork. The caller was Mark Gurdon, twenty-eight, manager of the Sturgis estate agency in Fulham Road in west London, where Susannah had worked for sixteen months. 'I don't want to worry you, Mrs Lamplugh,' said Gurdon. 'But we've got a bit of a problem. Has Susannah had lunch with you?'

Those words were quite enough: already Diana Lamplugh feared that something terrible was unfolding in their lives. She listened with mounting anxiety as Gurdon relayed what had happened. It had been a routine Monday morning in the office, and amid general banter Susannah had been making phone calls about a cheque book, pocket diary and postcard she had lost the previous Friday. She took some phone calls from clients as well, and had left the office just before lunchtime on a routine house-showing call – clutching the particulars and keys of 37 Shorrolds Road, a furnished, three-storey terraced house that only days before had come on to the Sturgis books for £128,000. That week, the house was being advertised in the *Fulham Chronicle*.

The estate agent manager remembered Susannah coming behind his desk to pick up the keys, which were attached to the large and distinctive yellow Sturgis key fob. The drive from the office to the house would have taken, he estimated, between

6

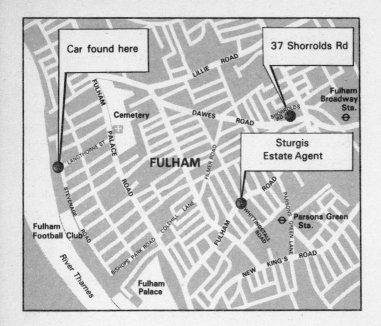

Car found here

37 Shorrolds Rd

LILLIE ROAD

FULHAM PALACE ROAD

Cemetery

DAWES ROAD

SHORROLDS RD

Fulham Broadway Sta.

LANGTHORNE ST

FULHAM

FILMER ROAD

Sturgis Estate Agent

STEVENAGE ROAD

BISHOPS PARK ROAD

COLEHILL LANE

FULHAM

WHITTINGSTALL ROAD

ROAD

PARSONS GREEN LANE

Parsons Green Sta.

Fulham Football Club

River Thames

NEW KING'S ROAD

Fulham Palace

three and four minutes. He would have expected her to return straight after the appointment, probably bringing a sandwich back to the office for lunch. She was ambitious and always keen to take phone calls that might lead to more percentage commissions for her.

By the middle of the afternoon, Gurdon told Mrs Lamplugh, he and his colleagues were concerned. It was very unlike Susannah to take long, unauthorized lunches. They went to where she sat – Susannah was the most attractive woman on the staff, and had been given the desk nearest the window – and found in her desk diary the words '12.45 Mr Kipper – 37 Shorrolds o/s', a routine entry implying that she was showing a client called Mr Kipper that particular house, and meeting

7

him first outside. She had taken only a purse with her, leaving her handbag by the desk: further evidence, if any was needed, that she intended to be out for only a matter of minutes.

'Have you checked hospitals? Been back to the house? Told the police?' Mrs Lamplugh fired at Gurdon. He had indeed been back to 37 Shorrolds Road with a colleague, but had found no sign of Susannah in or out of the house, and no indication either that anything was amiss. But a neighbour at number 35, a fifty-eight-year-old unemployed bachelor named Harry Riglin, had told them he saw a young man and woman leaving number 37 next door and looking up appraisingly at the house as they did so: possibly a young couple buying a house, he had thought idly. The young man was handsome, twenty-five to thirty, 5 feet 8 inches tall, medium height, clean shaven with thick combed-back dark hair, and looked prosperous in a smart dark suit. He had taken less notice of the woman.

All this worried Gurdon. Whatever had happened, he reasoned, must have occurred after Susannah met this mysterious 'Mr Kipper'. He knew of no Sturgis client of that name, but this was by no means unusual – the man might have phoned only that morning, or even come into the office, and there were far too many clients for him or anyone else to keep track of every one. Nevertheless it was by now clear to Gurdon that something had gone very, very wrong. He would go to the police himself to report that one of his staff called Susannah Lamplugh – 5 feet 6 inches tall, of medium build and with blonde-streaked hair, wearing a peach blouse, black jacket and grey skirt, two rings and low-cut stiletto-heeled shoes – had simply disappeared off the face of the earth.

Mrs Lamplugh's first reaction was to phone her husband Paul, who worked for the Law Society in central London. But he had already left for home. She tried Richard, Susannah's brother, who was a year older and who ran a fish farm in Hertfordshire. But she could not get through to him: a combination of nerves and dyslexia, which had dogged all her children too, meant that she could not get the numbers right as she dialled. Her fingers would not do what her brain wanted them to do. Her two other daughters were away in New Zealand, but she finally contacted Doug Williams, an old schoolmate of Richard and a member of Susannah's social set. He too had not heard from Susannah, although he promised to ring round friends to see if anyone had any news. She left a message too on the answerphone of Michael Hough, a twenty-six-year-old insurance broker and former lover of Susannah who was still friendly with the Lamplughs. Then Gurdon rang back: alas, there was still nothing at all to report.

An hour later, Paul Lamplugh began the daily commuter's evening trudge from Mortlake station he had followed for seventeen years: down from the station, across Upper Richmond Road, then home to suburbia in East Sheen Avenue. He had long since known his wife was prone to dramatization, but as soon as he saw her he realized that something very serious had happened: 'We've got a problem,' she told him as he entered the front door. 'Suzy hasn't come back from work.' He went white with shock, and from that moment realized that something terrible had happened – even fearing at some level that his eldest daughter was already dead. But he knew he had to be serious, calm and rational: not to panic, to work out what needed to be done.

Gurdon, meanwhile, had been phoning the Charing Cross and St Stephens hospitals: no, no Susannah Lamplugh had been admitted after any accident. He went to Fulham police station to report the situation, but there was such a long queue he abandoned the idea and himself went to a house-showing appointment. Life had to go on. When he returned to the office he tried ringing the phone number of Susannah's flat, for she had lived away from her parents' home for six years. But there was no reply. He returned to Shorrolds Road: still nothing.

Exactly six hours after Susannah left the Sturgis office, PC Duncan Parker answered the phone at Fulham police station: 'Can I help you?' At the other end was a breathless Gurdon, now officially informing the authorities of Susannah Lamplugh's disappearance. The call was logged at 6.45, and an officer phoned Gurdon back at 6.55 for more details. He recounted to the police an outline of what had happened, adding that Riglin now thought that the young couple had been arguing and was saying that the woman was bundled into a car by the man. This later turned out to be an exaggeration, but it was enough to make the police act immediately.

Within ten minutes established police procedures slipped smoothly into gear. Details were entered into the computerized police dispatch system. A description of the car Susannah used, and which she had presumably driven to her appointment – a white Ford Fiesta owned by Sturgis, registration number B396 GAN – was flashed to all cars, motorbikes and policemen on the beat in the area. The duty inspector, Ken Thompson, was alerted. So too was the Criminal Investigation Department at the station, and from there two plainclothes detectives were immediately sent to 'enter and search' 37 Shorrolds Road. Nothing of apparent relevance was found, but a constable was posted on guard duty outside. Two files – Misper Report FF584/1/54 and PNC W M No 139534C – were formally opened.

The next step was to contact a senior CID officer at home, so that he could take charge of what was already becoming a major investigation. That night, Detective Inspector Johnstone happened to be the officer on call for emergencies. In less than a week Johnstone, married with three young daughters, would be thirty-seven. He had been seventeen years in the police and was currently involved in the investigations into the murder of an elderly lady named Florence Tisdale – who had been raped and strangled the previous Wednesday, the day the rest of the world was watching the marriage of Prince Andrew and Sarah Ferguson in Westminster Abbey. The phone duly rang at nine that evening in Johnstone's Surrey home: 'A female', a voice announced in the unemotional, laconic tones of policemen everywhere, 'has gone missing.'

The situation was briefly outlined to Johnstone. 'Go to her home address immediately,' Johnstone ordered. 'Whatever you do, get in there.' He had to rule out the possibility that Susannah was at her flat in bed with a lover, oblivious to all the mayhem around her – or that she had simply gone home feeling wretched with influenza and had forgotten to tell anyone. Neither seemed likely but both had happened in other cases and so had to be eliminated as possibilities. 'And', said Johnstone, 'go back to Shorrolds Road too. Get uniformed to organize a street grid search for the car.' This was another practised police procedure, whereby each patrolling policeman was allocated a small section of the map and told to search methodically in that area.

To Johnstone, all the circumstances already added up to something decidedly sinister. It just did not sound right, an apparently normal and well-adjusted girl who went out at lunchtime without even her handbag – and never returned. He had been told about the apparent sighting by Harry Riglin too, and the struggle Riglin was supposed to have witnessed. Missing persons files are classified by police as either 'active' or 'non-active', but this was most definitely an 'active' case – one in which there were 'circumstances which must dictate suspicion'. He made the decision to return to London immediately, getting in his red Talbot Solara and speeding up the A217 towards Fulham police station.

Back in East Sheen, Paul Lamplugh downed a whisky and ate some food, intentionally keeping to a cool routine. He phoned the local Putney police station, who to his irritation did not seem to share his urgent view of the matter. So he got into the MG sports car outside – a two-seater 1972 GT model he had recently given his wife – and set off himself for Fulham police station. He left his wife sitting in their front living room, numb with shock – but they realized that someone had to stay at home in case Susannah tried to phone. She might be held prisoner somewhere and need help desperately, and theirs would probably be the first number she would try. Mrs Lamplugh busied herself polishing the furniture, pacing the floor, spreading paperwork over the floor.

Her husband duly drove over Putney Bridge north across the Thames, already going over in his mind what fate could possibly have befallen his daughter. Perhaps it was all some terrible misunderstanding. He joined another queue at Fulham police station – didn't they realize this was *serious*? – but soon found the policemen on the desk were taking the case extremely seriously. The two detectives who had been to Shorrolds Road had just received Johnstone's first order, and asked Lamplugh to go with them to Susannah's £70,000 top-floor, two-bedroomed flat in Putney, back south across the river. There, in time-honoured police fashion, one of them broke open the door with his shoulder. It was now dusk. The flat was completely empty, and there was no sign either of Susannah or her

12

flatmate, a twenty-five-year-old advertising executive named Nick Bryant.

The detectives quickly searched for any obvious messages that might have given some hint where, if anywhere, Susannah was planning to go that lunchtime. They looked for numbers on the board by the phone, but with no success. There was just a feeling of humdrum normality; probably after breakfast at around 7.45, she had left for work in her office Ford Fiesta and arrived in Fulham Road about 8.45. In her bedroom lay a half-finished dress, with an incomplete sleeve beside the sewing-machine her mother had lent her not long before. By this time Bryant had still not returned home, so the detectives secured the flat as best they could and drove off with Paul Lamplugh, vainly scouring the west London streets for any sign of official missing person number FF584/1/54.

They had been in the car for only minutes when they heard crackling over the radio the first significant news of the evening. Moments before 10 o'clock, PC Christopher Dollery, nearing the end of his 2.30–10.00 late shift, reported from his patrol car that he had found Susannah's vehicle. Johnstone's grid search had paid off. The Fiesta was parked facing north on the eastern side of Stevenage Road, a nondescript residential road about half a mile long, which motorists had used as a short cut to by-pass the busy Fulham Palace Road before barriers were erected to prevent them. For drivers, therefore, it was effectively not a through road. It ran parallel to the Thames, with Craven Cottage, Fulham Football Club's ground, and various wharves, warehouses and garages lying between it and the river.

But already detectives were faced with the first baffling mystery of the case: why was Susannah Lumplugh's car parked in a road leading nowhere, a good mile from the house she should have been visiting in Shorrolds Road and in the opposite direction from her office? Johnstone, by now taking command in Fulham police station, immediately gave orders that the car be forensically examined and photographed at first light in the morning. Police always follow the policy of assuming the worst in such an investigation: in this case, presuming from the beginning that Susannah had been murdered and that every piece of forensic evidence would be needed for a conviction if and when the murderer was caught.

In the meantime, another policeman would be posted at the car throughout the night – and one would be waiting too at the Sturgis office in Fulham Road, just in case Susannah turned up for work in the morning. Johnstone left to visit Shorrolds Road and Stevenage Road for himself, and asked the uniformed branch to start house-to-house inquiries near where the car was found. Even though it was already late in the evening, experience had shown time and again that this was the most effective way of gathering evidence in such circumstances. It was essential to strike immediately, to question people about what they had seen while it was still fresh in their memories. Even a day later, intelligent and rational people could get crucial times, dates and places hopelessly confused.

The two detectives with Lamplugh, hearing news of the find on their car radio, raced to Stevenage Road. Other police cars had reached the scene first; they were clustered around Susannah's car as they had come to a halt, the urgent jargon of radio operators blasting through open police car doors, the flashing blue lights on the roofs dramatically illuminating the pavement around them. Lamplugh was made to stay in the detectives' car while they assessed the scene. First, they soon decided, it seemed likely the car had been parked in a hurry: it was slightly askew from the pavement, and was overlapping the entrance to a garage by about eighteen inches. Second, the handbrake was off. Third, the driver's door was unlocked but the passenger's locked, suggesting immediately that only one person had driven the car to that place.

Detectives could make only a cursory examination of the car, because they had to be careful not to impede the work of the forensic scientists due to arrive at dawn. They could not afford to spoil any possible fingerprints, or remove hairs or fibres possibly even invisible to the naked eye. The car would probably be lifted and taken to the police forensic laboratories the next day, but in the meantime they had to establish there was no crucial evidence that could lead them immediately to Susannah. Extremely gingerly, they opened a door and lifted the luggage flap at the back to make sure nothing was concealed in the car boot. What they could see clearly was Susannah's straw hat on the back shelf; in the map rack in the driver's door, a purse. But by this time they had also noticed a fourth clue, and possibly the most significant. The driver's seat was pushed back from its forward position, the one any woman of Susannah's height and build would use. To the detectives the implication was all too clear: a *man* had driven Susannah Lamplugh's car to Stevenage Road.

The frustration, though, was growing for Paul Lamplugh. He was still waiting lamely in the police car, not allowed to come too close to his daughter's car lest he impede vital evidence. Already, his daughter and her belongings had become public property, and he was just a bystander – even though, just twenty-four hours before, he and his wife had bidden farewell to Susannah when she drove cheerfully from their house in this very same car. She had been to see her parents for an evening visit, and among the last words she had spoken to them were: 'Life is for living, you know.' Just as she left them she had remembered an interview Lamplugh was due to have

15

in a week's time, for another post at the Law Society, and wished him luck. Then she was gone. She had been alive, life was routine, ordinary – but in just a matter of hours there had been one of those awful transformations that come with sudden, unexpected trauma. He felt strangely dulled as he watched the police go about their work, reporting on their car radios, conferring about evidence. Didn't they realize this was his *daughter* they were talking about?

The police took him back to Fulham police station, where Mark Gurdon and Adam Leegood – a twenty-seven-year-old reinsurance broker and Susannah's current boyfriend – were also waiting. Leegood was the first man to be brought in for questioning: it is one of the more distasteful tasks for police in such a situation to have to interrogate first those close to the presumed victim, even though they may be more shocked and upset than anyone. But nine out of ten murders are committed by people known to the victim, and so for that reason alone Leegood automatically became the first suspect. It turned out he lived in a flat in Clapham, but that night was out dining with clients in central London. He returned to his flat just after 10.30 to be met by his flatmate, who told him that the police had been and were now wanting to see him at Fulham police station. It was extremely urgent.

He was there until 3.30, being gently but firmly interrogated in a bare interview room. Could he account for his movements during the day? If he had lunch with anyone, what were their names? Did he have colleagues who could vouch for his presence in his office during the day? What business meetings did he have? What was his relationship with Susannah? Had he had any recent disagreements with her? Had he, in fact, anything to do with her disappearance? Patiently he recounted his day: he had reached the office at about nine, and had meetings during the morning, one out of the office. He went to lunch with a woman friend in her company's dining room in the City, and more meetings throughout the afternoon. He stayed in his office until seven, whence he left for the prearranged dinner.

That afternoon he had tried to phone Susannah at Sturgis at 4.45, and left a message. He had last spoken to her on the phone at 10.15 the previous evening after she returned to her flat from seeing her parents, and was due to go to a party with her the next night. He had known her for eleven months, but had been her lover for only three. He was a member of the so-called Putney Set, and like Susannah was an enthusiastic windsurfer. He had a good relationship with her, and had no idea what could have happened. Nothing was amiss when they had spoken on the phone the previous evening. Business contacts, friends, were all duly noted down by police: all would be thoroughly checked, though no one had any reason to suppose Leegood was anything other than innocent. It would nevertheless take a lot of work, and eleven statements from others, before he could be positively and formally eliminated from the inquiry into Susannah's disappearance.

The other key person who had to be regarded as a suspect until proved otherwise was Nick Bryant, Susannah's flatmate, who paid her £150 a month for the second bedroom in her flat. That evening he had been at the Hand in Hand pub on Wimbledon Common, drinking with fellow Essex University graduates. He returned home to the flat in Putney at about 11.45, only to discover a message that the police had broken in. Susannah had not returned, but that was not necessarily unusual. He then gave detectives an account of *his* movements: that evening he had also been looking at a house he was interested in buying. No, he had only a platonic friendship with

Susannah though he regarded himself as a friend rather than lodger. He did not know of anyone who wished her any harm, though she *had* told him about strange phone calls she had apparently been receiving a couple of months before. And no, Susannah was most definitely not the sort of person to take off without first telling anyone.

With all this urgent activity going on around him, Paul Lamplugh was becoming frustrated inside Fulham police station. He had been sitting uselessly in a bleak interview room for what seemed to him an eternity, apparently having only an unimportant walk-on role in something which was so central to his life. He was especially fond of his eldest daughter and, as with his other children, night after night had helped her overcome her dyslexia by coaching her successfully through her O-levels. Perhaps there could still be a rational explanation for what had happened, and all would be well . . . But he was only a nuisance here, he decided, and there was depressingly little news. It was time to go back to his wife, vainly waiting in East Sheen for the call that might be from Susannah.

Detective Inspector Johnstone had himself questioned Leegood, but was now shuttling between Shorrolds Road and Stevenage Road. The first priority was to organize a 'walking street search' in the area where the Fiesta was found. Ten police constables, two sergeants, Johnstone himself and three CID dog-handlers with their Alsatians started methodically searching the gutters, the river bank, the towpath, a nearby luxury block of flats, and garages in the area around Stevenage Road. It was dark and they could see little, but there was no time like the present for such work: it was beginning to rain, and a rainfall could wash away vital evidence.

Paul Lamplugh meanwhile arrived back in East Sheen to discover his wife watching television, still desperately focusing her mind on something. She felt a great urge to *do* something too. It was now 12.30 in the morning, but she decided there was no choice but to take the matter into her own hands. She would find Susannah herself. Her husband loaded their two dogs – an ageing black cocker spaniel called Snoopy and a golden retriever, Leo – into the car, and they set off once again back across the Thames towards Stevenage Road. They soon saw Susannah's car, now guarded by a lone uniformed constable, and decided to walk down an opening from Stevenage Road that went to the Thames.

The dogs, they hoped, might be able to pick up Susannah's scent. In the early hours of the morning it was eerily quiet down by the river; the tide was half out, and it was now drizzling. The Lamplughs walked up and down the towpath, convincing themselves that their daughter must be close, possibly imprisoned in one of the scores of lock-up garages. They peered into back gardens, opened shed doors, the trusty family pets by their side aware only that something they could not comprehend was happening. In desperation Diana Lamplugh started to shout for Susannah: 'Suzy. Suzy. SUZY!' Her voice carried over the empty and silent Thames, amplified by the still night air. But there was no answer.

The commotion by the river's edge, meanwhile, had caught the attention of the police engaged in their methodical search, and Detective Inspector Johnstone came over to the Lamplughs and introduced himself. The Lamplugh dogs, he told them politely, were hampering the professional police dogs in their search and confusing scent patterns. He totally understood their desire to do something, but felt it would be better for all concerned if they went home and got some sleep. They found that prospect difficult: their adrenalin was flowing and they felt, in Diana Lamplugh's words, as though they were 'on fire'.

But reluctantly they agreed to return home, where Paul had his nightly whisky and Diana her vodka and lime. Then they fell fast asleep soon after three a.m.

For the detectives, there was to be no sleep that night. Two more key figures had to be brought in to complete the team. Shortly after one o'clock Johnstone had woken Detective Sergeant Barley, who was also at home, in Surrey, to ask him to come in to the police station to become 'manager' of the inquiry. Such modern corporate terminology had only recently become part of police parlance. Barley's job would be to supervise the running of the inquiry office and make sure all its paperwork was kept in order: a crucial job, because streamlined administration meant streamlined thinking in an inquiry of this kind. He was thirty-one and engaged to a woman detective constable; he had been twelve years in the Metropolitan Police and had spent many hours as a uniformed sergeant in the North and Midlands dealing with demonstrating coal miners during the National Union of Mineworkers' strike two years before. He too rushed to Fulham police station.

To complete the police procedure, a detective superintendent from the area's headquarters was also needed, to become the 'Senior Investigating Officer'. Fulham fell in Six Area, one of eight bureaucratic divisions of London's police, and this was going to be an 'AMIP' case – an area major investigation controlled from Kensington, rather than Fulham police station. Most cases they dealt with there were murders, rapes or major robberies, and Johnstone was already working with them on the Florence Tisdale murder.

The name of a senior officer on stand-by happened to be written in felt-tipped pen on the laminated boards the detectives used for messages, and that name was Detective Superintendent Carter. For no better reason, he was the senior officer contacted, though no one realized at the time that the choice was poignantly appropriate. Three years before, his mother-in-law had mysteriously disappeared in the Himalayas and never reappeared. He was forty-eight, married with two young children, and due to retire from the force in just five months, after twenty-nine years – eight of them with Criminal Intelligence in Scotland Yard, where he targeted major criminals. He had been in charge of nine murder investigations, all of which were solved. His wife and two children were already in Somerset, anticipating his retirement, and he was living on his own in a west London bedsit.

His summons meant that by the middle of the night, the three men who would lead the hunt for Susannah had been chosen. For many months to come – far longer than seemed conceivable that night – their lives would be haunted by the baffling case of Susannah Jane Lamplugh, missing female. They would get to know virtually everything there was to know about her; her likes and dislikes, her habits, attitudes, movements, even her thinking.

They were actually building such a dossier already. By the time Diana and Paul Lamplugh fell into a surprisingly sound sleep back in East Sheen, more than 500 police manhours had already been devoted to a fruitless search for their daughter. The mystery about what had happened to Susannah Lamplugh after she left her office at 12.40 that Monday lunchtime was deepening by the hour.

Chapter Three

The only consolation for the Lamplughs when they woke at dawn next morning was that everything that could be done was being done. Detective Superintendent Carter, the Senior Investigating Officer, was in Fulham police station shortly after six. Detective Inspector Johnstone, Investigating Officer, and Detective Sergeant Barley, Inquiry Manager, had already spent a sleepless night co-ordinating the search for Susannah.

More dogs and their handlers moved in at first light, and thorough daylight searches of the areas around Shorrolds Road and Stevenage Road were soon under way. The River Police were called in to search the Thames and its banks. The Mounted Branch and even a police helicopter were diverted to help. A hapless young detective who had of late been unpopular at the station was appointed 'Drains Officer', ordered to examine minutely the surrounding drains and sewers for any conceivable clue. If Susannah had been kidnapped, for example, her assailant might have dropped down the nearest drain her car keys, or the keys to her flat – for these had disappeared with her. So had the Sturgis keys to 37 Shorrolds Road and the particulars of the house.

But the drains yielded nothing, nor did a search of gardens and open spaces in the vicinity. Even Barnes Common, across the Thames, was carefully scrutinized by the dogs, the Mounted Branch, and the helicopter – with no success. A police photographer took pictures of Susannah's office Ford Fiesta, still parked in Stevenage Road, from every conceivable angle. An artist (who ironically lived close to Susannah's flat in Putney) was briefed by police to provide an artist's impression of 'Mr Kipper', the supposed Sturgis client whom Riglin thought he had seen in Shorrolds Road.

House-to-house inquiries were resumed at seven. It was essential to find potential witnesses before they left for work, and while the events of the previous day could still easily be recalled. The River Police, meanwhile, were providing some grim expert advice. If they were to assume the worst – that Susannah had been murdered and then thrown in the Thames – current tides and river movements meant that her body would take three or four days to surface. Then, they thought, it would probably appear several miles downriver, east of Fulham and somewhere in the Wapping area.

But events were moving fast elsewhere. The Fiesta, instead of being examined *in situ*, was being lifted on to a police vehicle and taken direct to the Metropolitan Police forensic laboratories in Lambeth, in south London. There a detective sergeant was appointed 'Exhibits Officer', immediately taking charge of Susannah's belongings from the car – the straw hat and her purse, which turned out to contain £15 and credit cards. The car was then subjected to the most stringent forensic tests available, using laser technology. Fingerprints were first taken, though at this stage nobody could distinguish between which were Susannah's prints, or Adam Leegood's, or those of some other legitimate user of the car. There seemed nevertheless to be two or three interesting discernible prints, a partial palm smudge on the car's rear-view mirror and a fingerprint on the windscreen seven inches from the nearside.

Then 'sweepings', whereby minute debris is retrieved from the scene of a crime, were taken from the car floor and sealed in plastic bags. 'Tapings', where special adhesive tape is attached to upholstery such as car seats and then peeled away with whatever microscopic material might attach itself, were also carried out. The theory behind such forensic examination is straightforward: that anybody who has been at the scene of a crime will inevitably leave *something* behind whether they realize it or not, be it hairs, infinitesimal fibres from a jacket, or even skin. The evidence became the responsibility of the Exhibits Officer, ready if it was ever needed for a trial.

Back in Fulham police station, the three key detectives held an early-morning strategy meeting and decided to set up an incident room on the station's second floor. This was a major step because it needed a minimum of nine officers to function satisfactorily – some to answer the phones, others to act on incoming information and allocate duties to detectives, and still more to embark on the laborious process of indexing every remotely useful fact in the case. The procedures for a major inquiry had been established since a series of murders of women in the north of England by Peter Sutcliffe, a psychopath who became known as the Yorkshire Ripper. Because neighbouring forces had not then cooperated as fully as they might, new standardized forms were brought in for all police forces so that work carried out by one force would be immediately comprehensible to another.

So Detective Sergeant Barley cleared his desk of all outstanding work, and set up a revolving carousel for the index cards in the new incident room. He arranged for a bank of phones to be brought in. Already the indexers, mainly women detective constables who had received special training for such a task, were at work – meticulously listing on separate index cards all possibly relevant scraps of information, then cross-referencing their work by filling out corresponding cards under other broad headings, and finally filing all the cards alphabetically. It was vital but unglamorous work: one error could be crucial if two pieces of apparently unconnected information were not linked by the system in the way intended. The same process could be carried out much more speedily on a computer, but only a few of the indexers had received the necessary training.

Meanwhile two young detectives were sent to the Prince of Wales pub in Putney, where Susannah's cheque book, pocket diary and a postcard were waiting. Was this significant? The landlord had found them the previous Friday night, soon after Susannah had apparently dropped them after having dinner with Leegood at Mossop's restaurant in Upper Richmond Road. The publican contacted her bank on Monday morning, who duly rang her at Sturgis. She then spoke to the landlord's wife at around 12.40 that lunchtime – in other words, immediately before she left the office – and arranged to pick them up at six o'clock on Monday evening. But she never turned up. The diary was important to the police, because it might contain crucial names and personal appointments. It was duly collected and rushed to the investigating team.

What they needed to know more than anything was where Susannah had gone the moment she stepped outside the door of the estate agency. Did she actually go to her car parked in Whittingstall Road, as colleagues supposed? Did she then drive it away? Did she really go to Shorrolds Road? Was Riglin's recollection accurate? Was it a genuine appointment with 'Mr Kipper'? Or did she make up the name because she was up to something she did not want her office to know about? If so, was it personal or professional? If she did meet 'Mr Kipper', where?

By mid-morning of Day Two all these questions had suddenly became very pertinent – for the house-to-house inquiries had yielded some remarkable information which turned all the previous assumptions upside down. It came from

25

Wendy Jones, a twenty-seven-year-old housewife who lived with her husband and two children at 123 Stevenage Road, the other side of the road from where Susannah's Fiesta had been found. The Joneses were trying to sell their house through Susannah's estate agency, and there was a Sturgis 'For Sale' sign outside.

Standing on her doorstep, Mrs Jones told a policeman that the previous day she took her dog for a very brief walk at about 12.40 p.m., then returned the animal to her house before calling for a neighbour, Ann Mahon. She noticed as she did so that a white Ford Fiesta was parked by the Mahons' garage, slightly overlapping the entrance, and she wondered whether Mrs Mahon's husband Leo would have difficulty getting his car into the garage that evening.

The two women then drove to the National Westminster Bank by Fulham Cross, where Mrs Mahon was changing a large amount of coins from the pay phone in her house. She was embarrassed taking so much time doing this when there were other lunchtime customers waiting behind her. She glanced at the bank clock and noticed it was 12.49. A couple of hours later Wendy Jones returned from shopping and saw the white car still there, still overlapping the driveway to the Mahons' garage by a few inches. She was certain it had not moved, she told the detectives. Later that evening she went to the cinema, and when she returned at about 10.30 the car was not only still in the same place but by now police were swarming around it too.

If Wendy Jones's evidence was correct, then Susannah's car was parked in the position in which it was found *from almost the moment she left the Sturgis office in Fulham Road* – well away from the house in Shorrolds Road. Police quickly established that Wendy Jones and Ann Mahon were reliable and level-headed women who were able to give accurate timings for their movements. They even checked the bank clock, and found that to be accurate too. It was devastating information. It cast doubt on whether Susannah had been to Shorrolds Road at all, because if she really had left her office at about 12.40 she could not possibly have had time to drive there, show a client a house, then get to Stevenage Road a mile away by 12.45.

But why was the car in Stevenage Road in the first place, unlocked and with Susannah's purse inside? Had she some business there no one knew about? Was it anything to do with the Joneses' house that they were trying to sell through Sturgis? Could it have been her whom Riglin saw outside 37 Shorrolds Road around one o'clock if her car had already been in Stevenage Road for a quarter of an hour and had not been moved since? Or *had* the car been moved between Wendy Jones's sightings of it at 12.45 and 10.30 and then returned to the identical place? It seemed highly unlikely, but not impossible. Had someone given her a lift to Shorrolds Road? The mystery was deepening all the time.

Johnstone, studying all the incoming information in the new incident room, was as baffled as anyone by this turn of events. 'This is going to be a "timings" inquiry,' he predicted to his colleagues. Everything seemed to hinge on the times: exactly when Susannah left her office, what time her car was parked in Stevenage Road, when she might have been in Shorrolds Road. With no other firm evidence, the only course was to retrace her movements and proceed doggedly like any such police inquiry – working out in conjunction with Susannah's movements who was where when, and gradually eliminating people until one suspect stood out. That was the hope, anyway.

The first essential information had come from Susannah's colleagues at the Sturgis office. There was no doubt that

Susannah had arrived at the estate agency at about 8.45. A few minutes earlier, eighteen-year-old James Calvert, the office junior, had arrived to open the front door to a new week's business. Susannah walked in next, followed by four of her colleagues: Gurdon, Nigel Hindle, twenty-three, Stephanie Flower, twenty-two, and a twenty-five-year-old temporary secretary from Australia, Kathleen Reidy. Susannah made them all tea just after nine, and Stephanie Flower thought she seemed in a particularly good mood. She was preoccupied with her missing cheque book, diary and postcard, first stopping the cheques with her bank and then (when she learned her belongings had been recovered) arranging to pick them up from the Prince of Wales pub that evening.

Calvert told the detectives that at about 9.45 he borrowed Susannah's Ford Fiesta to take a client to a house in Foskett Road, returning twenty minutes later and parking the car in Whittingstall Road, a street off Fulham Road and opposite the Sturgis office. Because Calvert was a small man, he used the same driving position in the car as Susannah – the seat about four or five notches back from its most forward position. It was not unusual for him to borrow someone else's office car, because one of his duties was to photograph all Sturgis houses on the market in the area – and he did not have a car of his own.

For the rest of the morning Susannah did not leave the office, the colleagues reported. Soon after midday she and Hindle and Flower went to the back section for a smoke (something Susannah could not bring herself to do in front of her parents). She shared her cigarettes with the others. Flower then left to show a house to a client. Reidy went out to her bank at 12.30 but returned five minutes later, and remembered seeing Susannah on the phone and half-sitting on her desk as if she was about to leave. She went to pick up the keys to 37 Shorrolds Road from the key board behind Gurdon's desk, and then took the house's details from a drawer. Everything seemed normal. She was carrying her purse too, and a ring holding the keys of her car, the office and her flat. Hindle recalled that as she went out the door she turned back to ask Calvert: 'Where did you say my car was?' And then she was gone.

It was unusually little for the police to go on. What was especially frustrating was that no one could establish whether or not 'Mr Kipper' was a real customer. The normal procedure when any new client phoned or called in at the Sturgis office was for the negotiator immediately to pull out a card and fill out details of the client's requirements – location, type of property, price willing to pay, and so on. But Susannah had filled in no such card for a 'Mr Kipper'. Did this mean that she had made up the name herself, and was never actually going to meet a client so named? Or merely that the man had contacted her at the last minute so that she had not had time to fill out a card? To complicate matters, someone had already told police that Susannah was dyslexic. That opened the possibility that she could simply have misspelled the name a man had given her. Perhaps it was a complicated foreign name that only vaguely sounded like Kipper – or even nothing like Kipper at all.

There was only one course open to the police, Detective Superintendent Carter decided. Faced with this confusing and limited dossier of information on what could have happened to Susannah, he felt that all he could do was to call for witnesses to come forward – and that meant bringing in the media to publicize the case. It was always a risk, because mass publicity could mean that a public eager to help in a baffling case would clog up the phone lines – and that was of no use to anyone. Every lead given by the public then had to be followed up, and that took vast manpower. Most of them would invariably be useless, but on the other hand it took only one to lead to success. He would also release the artist's impression of 'Mr Kipper' to the press, and the local newspapers would probably be happy to print it.

That morning, *The Standard* in London (later to revert to its original name of the *Evening Standard*) had picked up the story: 'A young woman estate agency negotiator', it reported dispassionately in a short news item, 'has vanished after taking a client to view a house in London.' Carter lifted his phone and dialled the number of Steve Wilmott, one of the police press officers. He outlined the story and then ordered Wilmott: 'Fix up a press conference for this afternoon.' Wilmott's response was so prophetic it would be recounted for months to come. 'I think', he told Carter, 'that the press will go big on this.'

Four miles away in East Sheen, Paul Lamplugh decided to go to work as normal. There was nothing he could do at home, he thought, and he had a lot of work at the Law Society – working on new practice rules for solicitors and preparing for his major job interview the following week. He had not been there long, however, when his phone rang. It was the police, asking him to come to a press conference at three o'clock in Fulham police station. Lamplugh had not told anyone in his office how his world had shattered, but now said quietly to his secretary: 'My daughter's been kidnapped.' He told his boss too, then set off for Fulham police station by underground.

He crossed the road for the short walk to the police station and was astonished by what he saw when he walked in the entrance in Heckfield Place. There was not just a handful of local newspaper journalists, but more than a dozen people congregating outside with notebooks and flashing cameras – most of them, he was told, from *national* newspapers. His wife and Adam Leegood were already there. To Lamplugh the atmosphere was expectant, even jokey, and Wilmott, the press officer, warned them: 'Don't smile for the cameras. It would look bad.' Lamplugh found he switched easily into what he called his 'matter-of-fact mode', a lawyer's detachment and insistence on staying with the facts and not becoming too emotional. He found time to think it absurd that the press was clamouring for pictures of these three previously unknown people.

They were taken to the station canteen, where the press conference began. 'What was your daughter like?' someone asked. 'Suzy', Lamplugh replied, 'was just an ordinary girl.' He meant it as a compliment to his daughter – that there were no hidden reasons, like drugs or mental instability, to explain her disappearance. But immediately something happened which would set the tone for the blitz of publicity to come. 'No, she isn't,' Diana Lamplugh suddenly, dramatically contradicted her husband. 'She's not ordinary at all. She's a *super* girl.' The press loved it, for this was the kind of copy which brought a human tragedy to life. Colourful quotes like that helped lift a fairly routine news story to a great human drama that could be spread across the tabloid pages. And Diana Lamplugh, desperately wanting her daughter back, somehow knew just that. In the months to come she would prove she had an unerring ability to deal with the media.

It was a warm summer afternoon, and later everyone went out into the station yard. There, under a hot sun, the Lamplughs and Leegood gave separate interviews. They were already on their way to becoming media personalities, and despite the pain of the afternoon Diana Lamplugh was somehow instinctively able to say all the right things. 'She's very lovely. Please let her go,' she told the reporter from the *Daily Mirror* to pass on to the mysterious 'Mr Kipper'. What she said was just what was needed to help get the story on to the front pages and alert the nation in the hunt for Susannah.

The three found the experience strangely stimulating, even slightly exciting, the adrenalin that comes with such drama coursing unexpectedly through them. That made the Lamplughs feel guilty, but they knew why they were giving the interviews: to find Susannah. Lamplugh realized later that the lightheartedness at the press conference, the strange detachment they felt, was a form of psychological protection from horribly stressful circumstances. Afterwards they briefly returned to anonymity and travelled home. They watched commuters, their lives no different from any other nightly routine, casually reading about a missing estate agent negotiator called Susannah Lamplugh, twenty-five. The commuters did not seem unduly affected by the news. 'Don't they realize this is our *daughter*?' the Lamplughs found themselves inwardly screaming once more.

They again slept well – but woke up on Day Three to find that literally overnight they and their missing daughter had become major nationwide news. The national newspapers had gone to town on the story. 'KIDNAP', the mass-circulation *Sun* splashed across its front page. 'House-sale girl vanishes on car trip with "client" ' – and there, beside a photograph of a Sturgis 'For Sale' board, was a 4 x 7½-inch picture of their daughter in a strapless party dress clutching a drink. *The Star* was equally bold on its front page. 'KIDNAP – Fears as sales girl Susie, 25, vanishes,' was the headline. 'A beautiful estate agent has vanished after showing a home to a mystery client. Last night fears grew . . .' The *Daily Mirror* selected an apparently spicy detail from Susannah's past: 'Beautician girl estate agent feared kidnapped.' Radio and television followed up the story on national news bulletins.

The Lamplughs had by now become public property. The realities of their situation and the fulsome fantasies of the tabloid press started to merge, and the two soon became indistinguishable. 'Suzy' – 'bright, white and professional' – became a 'vivacious' young woman who was 'full of life' and who always 'lived life to the full'. None of this was untrue, but it was an incomplete description of a sometimes troubled young woman who came from a complicated family. The media army, fascinating and diverting, came marching into the dreadful void of suffering and silence that had descended over 14 East Sheen Avenue the night before – welcomed and even fussed over in the Lamplugh household. The journalists, after all, were the people who might find Susannah. It was the start of a long and sometimes involved relationship between the Lamplughs and the media.

The phones were ringing by early morning: breakfast television, *News at Ten*, radio, newspapers, dismayed friends. Letters started arriving: 'Words cannot describe . . . I cannot say how sorry I am . . . how terrible for you.' Neighbours began knocking at the door, some tearfully mumbling their condolences while others offered food and flowers. By noon the front room was filled with flowers, the refrigerator packed with food. Mary Asprey – the forty-six-year-old wife of retired jeweller Harry Asprey and hitherto only a casual friend – turned up at the front door and was soon supervising the running of the household and answering the phone. Caroline Davies – a young freelance reporter working for *The Standard* – likewise knocked on the door with trepidation, but when she found herself welcome began a long and mutually fruitful relationship with the Lamplughs.

Next morning the phone continued to ring. One of the callers was John Bowron, Secretary General of the Law Society and Paul Lamplugh's boss, who suggested the family consult a top lawyer – maybe someone like Sir David Napley. Lamplugh duly phoned Napley, the seventy-one-year-old former President of the Law Society who was one of the best-known solicitors in the country. Napley immediately suggested that he and his wife have lunch with him. So, after less then forty-eight hours of the surreal whirl into which they had been plunged, Diana and Paul Lamplugh found themselves eating in a Chinese restaurant in Covent Garden with Sir David Napley and two of his partners. There was little substantial help Napley could give, but they found it helpful to talk to an authoritative, experienced, objective man. He did not think the idea of private detectives was a good one. He assured them of his concern, and said he was there if they needed more help.

Before long the Lamplugh parents were crossing London on an underground train with early homeward-bound commuters. Their daughter's picture was again splashed across *The Standard*'s front page, with the banner headline 'Divers join hunt for Susie.' They watched the faces of people reading Lamplugh's own words: 'We think she could be tied up somewhere, perhaps in a house, and somebody, somewhere must have some idea,' he was quoted as saying. 'Perhaps their neighbours have been acting suspiciously. It is imperative that they report it, even if they are wrong, because it could be our only hope.' But to all the other weary travellers it was just the news of the day, side by side with the cricket scores and details of how the Commonwealth was in disarray over South Africa.

To him that front-page story was central to the very core of his existence.

They arrived back to find a resolutely coping Mary Asprey at their front door. 'There are reporters all over the place. Most of them are in the garden,' she told them. 'One of them keeps going on about an exclusive.' In the back garden, with a bemused Snoopy and Leo playing host to the biggest influx of strangers the garden had ever known, were dozens of people – journalists, photographers, television crews. It was another warm and sunny day. The Lamplughs walked out of their French windows into the garden, and there was a sudden explosion of electronic camera shutters. 'There will be *no* exclusives,' Paul Lamplugh announced firmly. 'We will co-operate with the press if the press will co-operate with us.'

Now they were in demand by the media and were easily able to take control and dictate terms. But for a few seconds, for the first and last time, Diana Lamplugh lost her composure in public as the journalists were starting to leave. She saw Kay Burley, a reporter from the early-morning television station TV-am – and like some terrible mirage in the desert thought she had seen Susannah, suddenly returned home to the family back garden. All was well! Then she realized she was mistaken. 'I thought you were Suzy. *I thought you were Suzy*,' she said. 'You look so like her.' She turned tearfully back into the house, but moments later returned as composed and controlled as ever.

Even the police, meanwhile, were unprepared for the media barrage. Detective Superintendent Carter had in desperation organized press conferences before, such as one to appeal to witnesses to a homosexual murder to come forward. But on that occasion only the *Fulham Chronicle* had shown any interest. Now, because of the reaction, they were hurriedly having to install extra phones in the incident room, which were already ringing from dawn to midnight. No call could be ignored, not even the umpteenth member of the public telling them: 'Do you realize that if you take the "d" and "n" and "a" from kidnapper, you get "Kipper"?' The hundredth or even the thousandth such call might contain that vital information – and Barley especially started showing a prime quality needed for this type of investigation, an ability to be enormously patient with well-meaning but clueless members of the public. The television crews gathered obediently outside Carter's office, and at one point Johnstone had six radio reporters patiently waiting in a line to interview him.

Now the pressures on the police to solve this crime – if, indeed, there had been any crime – were mounting. They were coming not just from Susannah's family and their superiors in the Metropolitan Police. The media had joined the clamour, and that meant vast increases in the manpower necessary to deal with the resulting response. Until now detectives had concentrated nearly all their inquiries on a triangle – the Fulham Road office of Sturgis, Stevenage Road, and Shorrolds Road. They had attached a bug to the Lamplughs' phone line, so that any possible ransom calls could be recorded. But now, it seemed, there were millions of would-be detectives helping them around the country – and when countless old ladies were taking up valuable time by reporting that they had definitely seen 'Mr Kipper' on their bus, that was at times a mixed blessing. Not least because they *could* be right.

The missing Susannah Lamplugh was not the only pressing police matter, either. On the Tuesday evening, thirty-six hours since they had been to bed, Johnstone and Barley had gone home to snatch a few hours' sleep so that they could be up and fresh again on duty at 2 a.m. For weeks Johnstone had been planning the dawn arrest of twenty-six men working at the Blue Circle cement factory in Fulham, where employees were systematically stealing cement worth hundreds of thousands of pounds. The arrests needed at least fifty-two policemen, and notwithstanding his extra burden Johnstone decided to go ahead with the complex operation. It all passed off relatively peacefully on the Wednesday morning – Barley had been part of the arrest team too – but Johnstone and Barley had spent Day Three of the Susannah Lamplugh investigation dealing with the aftermath of this as well as the Lamplugh case.

Now they were able to devote all their time to finding Susannah Lamplugh. By now they knew, too, that there was another piquant personal reason why it seemed less likely that she had gone off on her own. Even though mother and daughter had a sometimes difficult relationship, it was almost inconceivable that on this day Susannah would not have found time to phone her mother. For Day Three had also been Diana Lamplugh's fiftieth birthday, and she had received no card or message from her eldest daughter.

Chapter Four

That evening the Lamplughs brought out champagne. Leegood and another friend of Susannah – Doug Williams, a twenty-six-year-old underwriter's assistant and founder of the Putney Set – joined them. They drank to Susannah and talked warmly about her and what could have happened. They also toasted Diana Lamplugh's *next* fifty years: none dare say the unthinkable, that Susannah might well by now have been murdered and her body dumped squalidly and unceremoniously in some unknown place.

Such thoughts, in the absence of any firm information on her fate, were simply too much to countenance. Her mother was sustaining herself by rushing busily around, taking Leo to the vet to have an injured paw bandaged, or her own mother to the hospital to have her eyes examined. People at the vet's wondered why she seemed so upset and was almost breaking down over her dog's paw. She was telling herself that maybe Susannah had been whisked off to somewhere like the Bahamas by Dave Hodgkinson – a former boyfriend with whom she had never entirely broken up. Hodgkinson, twenty-seven, was supposed to be in Corsica after finishing a job teaching sailing there the day before Susannah disappeared, but no one had been able to contact him since. Had he secretly returned to England and romantically invited Susannah to go away with him on the spur of the moment?

It was certainly not impossible – and even close family friends were among those convinced Susannah had gone off on her own and would return. The nation, too, was now divided about what could have happened to her. Her story was never off the tabloids' front pages, and even *The Times* printed large pictures of Susannah and the artist's impression of 'Mr Kipper' alongside each other. Diana and Paul Lamplugh found themselves rushed from one rival television studio to another, from TV-am to *Breakfast Time* – into a fast-moving new world of chauffeurs and limousines. The theories and rumours grew by the minute: word mysteriously spread around London estate agents that Susannah was really alive and well and living in Corfu.

There was, meanwhile, a dramatic development in East Sheen Avenue. A white Rolls-Royce pulled up and out stepped a twenty-nine-year-old American woman in floods of tears. She explained that her name was Pamela Spurr-Seager and that she had been a client of Susannah when she was working as a beautician in London four years before. Susannah gave both her and her property developer husband facials. She and Susannah had become friends and she had offered to put up most of the money for a beauty and fitness business which Susannah would run. They had not been in touch for some months until the previous week, when Spurr-Seager had phoned Susannah who immediately suggested lunch the following Monday. But that was the day off for the Spurr-Seagers' nanny, and she suggested the Tuesday instead. And now she blamed herself! If only she had agreed to go for lunch on the Monday, Susannah would be fine now! Diana Lamplugh was not there, and others found themselves comforting the distraught Californian.

But Spurr-Seager's information did give the police a clue. It proved that the appointment with 'Mr Kipper' had not been made more than a few days before, otherwise Susannah would almost certainly not have suggested lunch on the Monday. The

39

police took away every scrap of paper from Susannah's desk to try to find more information about her appointments, and twenty-eight-year-old Woman Detective Constable Barbara Harrison – who had spent two years on plainclothes surveillance duties, and who was known in the force for her strong Geordie accent – was given the task of painstakingly going through each entry in both her personal and professional diaries, so that everyone with whom Susannah came in contact could be followed up and investigated. It was an uphill task: at the time the Sturgis branch had on their books 232 male clients alone, and Susannah could have had dealings with any of them.

Already, too, the detectives were beginning the most delicate task of all: gently trying to discover the truth about Susannah's private life, her sexual contacts and her relations with her lovers, to see if any clues lay there. They soon established that she did not confine her sexual relationships to accepted boyfriends like Leegood, Hodgkinson and Hough – and that she had other lovers not known either to her family or the Putney Set. From friends and colleagues it quickly also became apparent that she was planning to end her relationship with Leegood. Details like this were important for the police, because by Day Four it seemed more and more likely that when Susannah left her office that Monday lunchtime, she was planning to meet someone she knew.

This was because information was coming in all the time from the house-to-house inquiries in Stevenage Road and Shorrolds Road, and not one person had reported seeing anything unusual or suspicious. Susannah was a fit young woman who would have put up a fight had she thought she was being abducted, the theory went: the fact that no one saw anything amiss during the middle of a busy summer day in London suggested she trusted the person she was seeing. A cab driver did report picking up a fare in Finlay Street (a turning off Stevenage Road), who told him he had seen a couple having a 'right ruck' – a fierce argument. (The fare, despite police appeals, never came forward.) Apart from this no one had actually *seen* anything. Two housewives separately reported hearing screams during the afternoon, one a 'spooky, high-pitched yowl' – but the school holidays were in full swing and there were dozens of children playing noisily nearby. And that was all: by hundreds of other accounts it was just a normal, peaceful day in Stevenage Road.

There were even two workmen digging holes and laying pipes in Stevenage Road, just yards from where Susannah's car was found, who testified to this. Either Bert Carter or his twenty-one-year-old son Christopher was working outside in the road all day, from nine to around four. But they neither saw nor heard anything remotely unusual, no screams, groans, shouts, struggles. Dozens of people had walked along the road, and they did not see or hear anything to report either. Several remembered seeing the parked white Ford Fiesta at various times in the afternoon or evening, and one schoolboy even claimed to have seen it around *midday*. Another cab driver, who lived in Stevenage Road, was certain he had seen the car in the position in which it was found when he parked his cab at around two o'clock. It now seemed beyond reasonable doubt that Wendy Jones was right – and that somehow Susannah's *car* had been parked in Stevenage Road only a matter of minutes after she left her office. But why? Had *she* been there too or not?

To add to the confusion, residents of Shorrolds Road were also reporting seeing nothing untoward. The apparently muddled Riglin was still certain that he had seen Susannah and a man in Shorrolds Road shortly before one o'clock – by which time, Wendy Jones was equally sure, her car was firmly parked in Stevenage Road, more than a mile away. Could both be right? Did Susannah leave her office earlier than the entire staff of Sturgis had estimated, and for some reason go from Shorrolds Road to Stevenage Road after her appointment? Did she have a genuine appointment in the first place?

Detectives knew that there was no office clock at Sturgis, so there was a slight possibility that all the staff there could have wrongly estimated the times. They also went back to Riglin, who seemed less sure of his story. A door banging that he said was number 37's could have been at another neighbouring house, he conceded when police checked with him. They also asked Adam Leegood to sit in Susannah's car, and he confirmed that the driving seat was not in Susannah's normal position. But meanwhile they had drawn a complete blank in the Fulham Road area. Not one single person who had seen Susannah leave the Sturgis office came forward, neither had anyone seen her go to her car parked by Calvert a few yards away in Whittingstall Road. She really seemed to have vanished from the moment she went through that door.

Two hundred policemen joined the searches by the end of the week - of every vacant property on estate agents' books in the area, of cemeteries, parks, and each of the forty acres of the Hurlingham Club. Local waterworks, BBC studios and even Fulham Football Club were among the places carefully scrutinized. Forensic experts concentrated their efforts on 37 Shorrolds Road but could find nothing incriminating, not even proof that anyone had been in the house that day. Its owner, a helicopter pilot working in Abu Dhabi, was questioned and cleared of any involvement. He had not even met Susannah Lamplugh. Susannah's dental impressions were obtained in case they were needed to identify a body, but every effort to find her blood group failed. Detectives visited 102 clubs, restaurants and wine bars in the Fulham and King's Road areas. Had a man possibly taken Susannah to lunch in one of them? But not one person had seen her.

The phones, though, were still ringing incessantly in Fulham Road police station. 'I think my husband is the man you're looking for,' several callers said. Police were fairly used to that type of call: often the women were seeking to have their husband questioned by police about the Lamplugh case, so they could then cite that fact in divorce proceedings. The wife of a doctor in Surrey reported very convincingly that her husband had returned home on the Monday afternoon acting suspiciously and with bloodstained clothing – and was now keeping a basement locked. A piece of paper saying 'HELP – Mr Kipper is holding me' was found west of London. All were conscientiously investigated, but turned out to be macabre false alarms or delusions.

Scores of people were also ringing in with alleged sightings of 'Mr Kipper' – in the north of Scotland, Wales, the Midlands. Others wanted to tell police what they thought 'Mr Kipper' meant, and Woman Detective Constable Harrison started card indexing 'Kipper - possible meanings'. Some thought it had something to do with the Yom Kippur holiday, others that it was connected with London cab drivers for whom 'kipper' is a slang expression for the slack season. There were also a handful of unfortunate people in Britain genuinely named Kipper – and their friends and neighbours were only too willing to tell the police about them. A lot of callers drew the attention of detectives to John Fowles's book *The Collector*, in which a man keeps a woman prisoner for months. 'Thank you very much for your help,' the detectives would say again and again. Then they would mark the paper detailing the call 'No further action'.

By Day Five the case was overwhelming Fulham police

station. There was simply not enough space for all the people needed to answer the phones, which were manned from eight in the morning until midnight. Whenever a call was finished that phone rang again immediately. So the inquiry team decided to move its operation to the AMIP's headquarters at Kensington, to the ground floor of a building next to Kensington police station. Here there were furniture, tables, space, chairs, filing cabinets in abundance. No fewer than four separate phone lines were reserved for press inquiries alone, for the mystery of what had happened to Susannah Lamplugh was fast becoming the most captivating news story of the summer. A major store in London ran out of women's 'shriek' alarms.

The massive publicity, the strange intensity of it all – the constant interviewing by journalists, the rushed visits to television studios, all the stimulus of new experiences – meant that back in East Sheen the Lamplughs still felt as though they were overheated. The strain was terrible, but to their surprise they slept well. In the first week they settled to the new routine of sleeping soundly, then waking at five and returning immediately to the question to which there was no answer. Just what had happened to their daughter? The two new members of the inner circle, Caroline Davies and Mary Asprey, arrived early each morning and went straight up to the Lamplughs' bedroom – where, sitting on the bed, they opened mail and discussed the latest developments in the case with Diana Lamplugh. Other neighbours turned up to give support and help with shopping, for Diana Lamplugh still felt unable to face local shoppers she might know.

By now their three other children all knew about the family crisis. But Richard, at twenty-six the eldest child and the one most affected by dyslexia, could not face talking about his missing sister and stayed in Hertfordshire managing the fish

44

farm. More than twelve thousand miles away, Susannah's two sisters – Tamsin, aged twenty-four, and Elizabeth, sixteen – had finally been contacted in Kaitaia, in northern New Zealand, and asked to phone home. Tamsin had left Britain for New Zealand the previous year to work for an international hotel agency, and Elizabeth had been rewarded with a holiday there by her parents for passing her O-levels. They had flown from Sydney to Auckland the day Susannah disappeared.

They had been tracked down to a camp site in Kaitaia where, in an emotional call – over an ancient telephone that had to be wound with a handle – Diana Lamplugh finally broke the news of how their sister had gone missing. Friends had been telling police in the meantime that Tamsin was Susannah's closest confidante, and detectives were now anxious to talk to both sisters in case they had vital clues – letters from Susannah, for example, in which she might have spoken of new boyfriends. But Elizabeth was bound for more holiday with family friends in Hong Kong before coming home – her trip had already been paid for – and Tamsin decided to return to her job in Auckland before making any decision to return to England.

Flowers, food, letters, were meanwhile tumbling in to the Lamplugh's London home every hour. Old friends and long-lost relatives, alerted by the media, were being rediscovered. Paul Lamplugh received a letter from his school matron at Cheltenham College (where his father was a housemaster). Tamsin's godfather resurfaced after being absent almost her entire life. Nearly all the letters read aloud around the bed in the early mornings expressed anguished goodwill, with many offering prayers too. 'We feel for you at this time of hardship and may everything turn up Rite for Suzy,' came one postcard from prisoners in the Isle of Wight. 'God bless you all from the Boys in D wing, Albany, Isle of Wight. We hate anything like

45

this happening. Us lot Maybe Rogues but we aint perverts. I hope you wont be offended getting a card from us.' Nuns wrote to say that they had lit candles for Suzy.

But the occasional letter was much less welcome. 'Susie had a fate worse than death. Come and see me and I will tell you all about it,' said one. The publicity soon attracted what seemed to be all the mediums, clairvoyants, dowsers and diviners in the country – and all were claiming some kind of divine knowledge about what had befallen Susannah. Some phoned and spoke directly to the Lamplughs or Mary Asprey, others wrote. Sometimes they spoke normally, at other times as though they were in a revelatory trance. They would always provide what the Lamplughs started to call 'Intelligence' about Susannah's movements, but it would invariably be hopelessly vague or incomplete. 'If you drive down a street in Fulham with a pub at the end of it . . . the street begins with an "M" . . . half-way down you will see houses boarded up,' was how one typical message went. 'That is where Suzy is, in one of those houses.'

Such calls, somehow both welcome and unwelcome, placed the Lamplughs in an unpleasant dilemma. It was all too easy to feel that the police were not doing enough. They had failed, after all, to find their daughter. The parents wanted to *do* something, something more than those steady, unrushed, laconic policemen – and who could say for certain that just one of these clairvoyants was not right? They simply could not tolerate the thought that because they had ignored one of these messages, they were failing to rescue Susannah. So Paul and Diana Lamplugh once again got into their MG sports car and drove across the Thames to Fulham, scouring the streets for the one the medium had apparently envisioned. A pattern developed. They would find a street, spot boarded-up houses, and then be able to do nothing about it – and they would shudder at the thought that their daughter might be lying in one of the houses. Police had soon searched all vacant houses in the area that were on estate agents' books, and found nothing.

A similar message from a clairvoyant before the end of the first week reported that Susannah was 'somewhere down by the river' – so with Mary Asprey, the Lamplughs spent a dark and overcast summer evening searching once again on the banks of the Thames. They found it eerie, opening the doors of empty sheds in the moonlight and hardly daring to think what they might find. Each time they peered into such a shed, the Lamplughs feared they might be faced with the body of their daughter. The three cut back surrounding undergrowth, beginning to be afraid as the night wore on that they might be attacked. They came across a building where a soccer club was holding a meeting, and Mary Asprey went in to tell them what they were doing. Paul Lamplugh told a man who came out to join the search: 'This would be extraordinary if it wasn't for the fact that I'm looking for my *own daughter*.' It all felt strangely clinical to him, almost as though he was looking for a dead animal. They searched more back gardens, and people came to ask what they were doing. 'Searching for Suzy, the missing estate agent,' the reply would come. Then they went home, and once again Paul and Diana Lamplugh quickly fell fast asleep.

But it was not just the well-meaning amateurs who were beginning to contact them. An agent claiming to represent Doris Stokes – a professional performer and 'medium' who held popular, profitable mass meetings in which she claimed to speak to the dead relatives of those present – unsuccessfully tried to strike up a deal with the Lamplughs. Then came a call from Uri Geller, an Israeli show business performer who enjoyed international acclaim for his ability to bend spoons, supposedly through his thoughts rather than actions. He now lived in Berkshire, but thought he could help find Susannah. He drove down the M4 in his Mercedes the Friday after she went missing, but even his premonitory powers did not enable him to find East Sheen Avenue and when he left the M4 he quickly became lost.

But he had a car phone and Paul Lamplugh guided him in. 'Come past the Chiswick roundabout and over the flyover,' he would say. 'You should just about be past Smith's Crisps factory now . . .' The Mercedes was directed to a road running parallel to the Lamplughs', and by coming in through a back-garden entrance Geller evaded the media pack encamped outside the front door. He had said he did not want any publicity while he was looking for Susannah. In the suburban front room he seemed an extraordinary figure: dressed entirely in saffron orange, and blessed with a strong belief, it seemed, that he really could find Susannah. He sat around a table with the Lamplughs; Diana Lamplugh also happened to be dressed in orange. He wanted something of Susannah's, possibly an item of clothing. Then he left, driving with Adam Leegood over what the Lamplughs were already calling 'the course' – the area between Shorrolds Road, Stevenage Road and Fulham Road.

And then, suddenly, Uri Geller had a vision. He spoke animatedly of Shell petrol drums, and drove back to Putney Bridge. He did a dramatic U-turn, and decided he had seen in his mind Susannah near a *warehouse* or *garage*. *Green doors* and a *blue car* were also somehow involved. Possibly a *uniform* too, and some kind of *journey*. That was all. Nothing more was coming, unfortunately. They drove back disconsolately to the Lamplughs, and Geller announced that he had done all he could do. He bent a spoon which was given pride of place on

48

the Lamplughs' mantelpiece until it was later stolen. Then he drove home to Berkshire. Six days later he phoned the house again: 'This is Uri. I think you need me to ring you.' He continued to talk to Mary Asprey – by now organizer of the mediums and clairvoyants – but was unable to provide any clues to find Susannah. Before the end of the following year he would tell a magazine that besides his spoon-bending activities, he now spent his time searching for gold, oil, diamonds and 'even for kidnap victims'.

The Lamplughs nevertheless derived hope from the attention of all the mediums and clairvoyants, both amateur and professional. They brought positive theories and ideas demanding action, while the police could bring no real hope at all. But already the input of information from the mediums was merging imperceptibly with that of the police – and it was not always easy for those involved to tell the difference. A medium would later claim, for example, that she sensed that one of Susannah's closest lovers was homosexual. This was not true, but it added another 'fact' to the feverish supply of theories and 'intelligence' that was fast beginning to swamp the household. The police could not supply Susannah – but the mediums could at least bring visions of her. To the Lamplughs and Mary Asprey, they had already become an important and intrinsic part of the investigation into Susannah's disappearance.

The official detectives were regular visitors to the house all this time. Detective Superintendent Carter had laid down the principle from the beginning of his career that policemen should always strive to keep the victims of crime informed about investigations – and whether there had been crime in this case or not, he, Johnstone and Barley were determined to keep in almost constant touch with the Lamplughs. A close bond between them developed almost immediately. When

Johnstone celebrated his thirty-seventh birthday at the end of the week, the Lamplughs sent him a bottle of champagne.

But the bad news came on Day Five from Detective Chief Superintendent David Lamper, the man in charge of all criminal investigations in west London. Like Geller, he came in to the Lamplugh house the back way, through the garden – in order to deliver what Diana Lamplugh later called 'obvious shock treatment'. It was the first time the police had confronted the Lamplughs with the hard realities that they had to face. There were now two realistic possibilities, said Lamper, a policeman of the old school: either Susannah had gone off willingly on her own, or she had been abducted. Either was possible, and the police had an open mind. If she had been abducted she would almost certainly now have been murdered too, which meant that her body would now be lying somewhere. *Both possibilities needed to be faced*.

The effect of such a talk was salutary, and Mrs Lamplugh later called it 'brutal'. Then came a curious and unexpected event – a lively gathering at the Lamplughs', held just five days after Susannah had gone missing. The momentum for it grew on the day. By early evening most of the Putney Set had decided, with mixed feelings, to come. It became almost a wake for Susannah, as well as an unexpectedly cathartic experience for all who attended: guilt evaporated, there was wine, animated conversation, even jokes. Dave Hodgkinson by now had turned up in London, and there was both relief and sadness that he did not somehow hold the key to Susannah's disappearance.

But there was also a serious side to the evening: its purpose was to help the police by prompting the memories of her friends. The detectives who had been invited to mingle with the guests were therefore determined to use the occasion to try to find out more about Susannah and her friends. Their inquiry was now inevitably destined to go backwards – to discover more about the weekend before Susannah disappeared, the weeks, months, even the years, preceding that Monday lunchtime. It seemed unbelievable, but Susannah had still been missing for less than a week. Previous boyfriends (perhaps someone with a grudge?), her life as a beautician and later as a masseuse, her family background – even her life below decks on board the *QE*2 as she sailed around the world – all would need to be relentlessly investigated. Somewhere, there had to be *something*, some clue that would explain this mystery. To this end one of Susannah's friends handed round pieces of paper at the party. 'The object of this exercise is to complete a diary of Susie's activities from December 1985 to Monday 28 July 1986,' he had written. Everyone was asked to write in details of when and where they had seen Susannah, and in whose company.

That spontaneous effort showed how the task awaiting the police was growing more formidable every day. But in the meantime they held what Diana Lamplugh called a 'brainstorming' session around the assembled guests. Each racked his or her brains in an endeavour to find that elusive clue. Everyone put forward their idea of what could have happened to Susannah, whom they thought she could have been with. Nobody liked to suggest anything other than that she was alive and well, that it was only a matter of time before she was back among them. Then it was the turn of Dr Desmond Kelly – a Harley Street psychiatrist and specialist in schizophrenia, depression and anxiety, who attended the same church as the Lamplughs and who was also present. He believed, he let it be known quietly, that Susannah had been abducted and murdered. He feared she was now dead. His words were chosen carefully, because he did not think it healthy that the Lamplughs or anyone else present should harbour false hopes for Susannah. He merely wanted to bring out into the open what most inwardly accepted by the end of the first week, that the outlook was now ominous.

Or was it? The detectives at the party that night already knew something that no one else there knew and which had suddenly changed the picture – for the previous day there had been a baffling development which had plunged the investigation into more confusion than ever. It was all so apparently contradictory that the police would not make public news of this development for weeks. What had happened was that a twenty-five-year-old woman, Barbara Whitfield, had come in to the police station and given detectives some astonishing information. She was a 'retained agent', she told the police, a person who looked for houses for clients who were too busy to look for themselves. Because of this work, she dealt continually with estate agents in the area and had come to know Susannah Lamplugh well – perhaps seeing her at least once a week on business.

The previous Monday, she told detectives, she left her office some time after 2.30 in the afternoon. She was on her bike, and cycled from Munster Road into Fulham Palace Road, through Fulham cemetery. And there – driving north towards Hammersmith in a white Ford Fiesta with a straw boater on the back sill – who did she see but her old friend Susannah Lamplugh. Next to her in the car was a man. She was looking serious but not particularly distressed, and did not notice that Barbara Whitfield had waved to her. Whitfield thought nothing more about it, until she realized that what she had seen might be relevant to the hunt for her.

It was not just relevant: it was utterly crucial. Barbara Whitfield was the first witness to report seeing Susannah who actually *knew* her, and therefore was much less likely to be mistaken. She was a sound, sane, well-educated professional woman. The police speedily checked with her colleagues that she had indeed made that journey on the Monday – and all confirmed that she had. Her evidence made nonsense of much of the information gleaned from both Shorrolds Road and Stevenage Road, and gave a new glimmer of hope for Susannah. If what Barbara Whitfield was saying was true, Susannah's car could not have been parked in Stevenage Road, in the position in which it was found, before mid-afternoon after all; the sightings by reliable people like Wendy Jones and her friend, and a London taxi driver, had to be wrong.

It meant, above all, that Susannah Lamplugh was alive and well and driving north up Fulham Palace Road in the middle of that Monday afternoon hours after she had apparently vanished. But was Barbara Whitfield right? What had become clear by now was that there were going to be no easy answers in this most perplexing of inquiries.

Chapter Five

The detectives were by now desperate for more information. 'Are you making any headway in this case at all?' Detective Superintendent Carter was asked by a television journalist. 'No,' he replied succinctly. 'I'm afraid we're not.' He still felt that the clues had to come from the public, which meant keeping media interest in the case so that possible witnesses would be encouraged to come forward. Publicity was proving anything but a problem, because even seven days after her disappearance the mystery of what had happened to Susannah Lamplugh was rarely absent from the nation's front pages or national radio and television news programmes.

The next step, the Lamplugh squad decided, was to stage a reconstruction of Susannah's likely movements to see if that could jog the memories of residents and passers-by. It proved difficult to find a policewoman near enough in appearance to Susannah to take her place, but finally – exactly a week after she went missing – Woman Police Constable Suzanne Long took Susannah's desk at the Sturgis office, watched over by television crews and photographers. Then, wearing clothes and jewellery similar to Susannah's, she got into a white Ford Fiesta in Whittingstall Road for the five-minute drive to Shorrolds Road. There Detective Sergeant Christopher Ball, looking as near as possible to Riglin's description of 'Mr Kipper', was waiting for her. So were uniformed policemen and women, stopping everybody to see if they could remember anything.

That night, too, Diana Lamplugh appealed on television for the return of her daughter. By this time her personality was already intriguing millions of television viewers, because there were none of the mumbling, inarticulate, tearful appeals usual in such cases. Instead, a confident Diana Lamplugh delivered her lines, measured and sometimes smiling, with all the ease of a seasoned television performer. She was always dressed brightly and smartly. There were no false starts, no breakdowns, no tears – not even any visible emotion or grief. It was so unusual a performance that it led many to ask what sort of woman Diana Lamplugh was. Could she be experiencing what psychiatrists call 'denial', whereby people under great strain are unable to face the realities of what is happening to them? Or, underneath the polished competence of her television appearances, was she really suffering as much as other mothers would in similar circumstances?

What was indisputable was that the personality of Diana Lamplugh was already one of the factors making the disappearance of Susannah such a unique case. Her tireless quest to find her missing daughter was having a major effect, for everyone seemed touched by the tragedy. Hundreds of young women disappeared every year but many received no publicity at all, and often there was little police effort to find them. But at least partly because of Diana Lamplugh's highly memorable television appearances, the media furore over this case intensified with a momentum all its own – and as a result so did the obligation on the police to solve the mystery. Very few murders, rapes or serious robberies received so much police time and resources. By the beginning of the second week, thousands of manhours had already been spent on a fruitless search for Susannah Lamplugh – and no one could really explain why.

The police investigation, though, was not yielding any significant new evidence. Detectives had no choice but to begin the painstaking task of piecing together Susannah's personal history in the hope that clues lay there, compiling a dossier listing all the milestones in one twenty-five-year-old life. Never before had one ordinary, innocent young woman's life become the subject of such intense police scrutiny.

The story of Susannah Lamplugh's life, it soon turned out, began on a dance floor in Cheltenham in 1952. The country was still in the grip of post-war austerity, and Sir Winston Churchill was to occupy 10 Downing Street for another three years. But Great Britain was in the throes of change: a new young queen would soon be on the throne and the nation would be drawn into its last great colonial expedition, the invasion of Suez. Compulsory National Service would end, with post-war austerity giving way to the self-proclaimed boom era of Harold Macmillan. The atmosphere on the dance floor ninety-seven miles west of London was excited: the boys of Cheltenham College, a fee-paying school in its 111th year, were being allowed to dance, under supervision, with local girls. But for a sixteen-year-old secretary named Diana Elizabeth Howell, it was not one of the public schoolboys who caught her eye.

The son of one of the school's housemasters – a twenty-one-year-old trainee London solicitor, home for the weekend, called Paul Crosby Lamplugh – seemed altogether more mature, more sophisticated, more handsome than the gauche young schoolboys. He offered to find her a second-hand car, which showed what a worldly young man he was. He turned out to come from a family which had been in England for almost nine hundred years; his ancestors had crossed the English Channel with William the Conqueror. They settled in a village in Cumberland called Lamplugh (pronounced 'Lampler'), and fast became known as the de Lamplughs. A member of the family became Archbishop of York in 1688.

But both Paul Lamplugh's parents were staunch Methodists,

and only when his father taught at Dartmouth and then Cheltenham did they convert to Anglicanism. They could not afford to send young Paul to university after his education at Cheltenham College, and instead he was articled to a London solicitor. He did his National Service in the army, becoming a training officer at Oswestry and ending up a second lieutenant.

His new girlfriend, he later learned, had been a 'difficult' pupil at school. Her family's background was Welsh. Her father was a local solicitor who had been injured at Dunkirk during World War II and ended the war as a War Office administrator, her mother a PE teacher whose career was curtailed by a car crash. She had a comfortable upbringing in Cheltenham: Diana and her three brothers went to private schools and enjoyed a tennis court in their back garden. But her earliest years were spent without a strong male presence, because her father was at war. She yearned as a child to be an actress, but found reading out loud difficult. (Dyslexia was later diagnosed in her children.) She finally left school at sixteen for a secretarial course, then travelled the country with a motorbike for eight months while working for a touring opera company. Later, media work at the BBC attracted her, and she worked as a secretary in the office of Kenneth Adam, a senior television producer and administrator, and in BBC women's television.

The young pair on the dance floor made an attractive couple. She was animated and outgoing, he much more shy and reserved. Both came from English middle-class stock, each aspiring to similar ideals and traditions. It was a sunny autumn day in Cheltenham when they married six years later, and the parish church was packed. Three hundred came to the reception at the Queen's Hotel. But the bride – who was prone to dramatic illnesses – became unwell just beforehand and travelled to their Paris honeymoon exhausted. Theirs had been a conventional middle-class courtship of the 1950s, and married life was a new experience for both. Following their honeymoon they returned to live in London. Lamplugh described his wife many years later as 'a wonderful wife'.

Susannah was the second of their four children, born after an especially trying pregnancy at her maternal grandparents' house in Cheltenham on 3 May 1961. It was a difficult birth, and the 10lb child emerged into the world with the umbilical cord around her neck. She was named Susannah after the actress Susannah York, who had just then made her first film and was becoming a celebrity. Susannah Lamplugh joined her brother Richard, who had been born sixteen months earlier. But she proved a difficult and highly active infant, crying constantly and rocking her cot – particularly at night. She did not like being cuddled, and pushed cooing adults away if she could. A sister, Tamsin, followed into the Lamplugh household fourteen months later. Elizabeth, the youngest, was born nine years after Susannah. Later the parents also acted as guardians to one of Paul Lamplugh's godchildren.

The new daughter came into a home already dominated by her mother. Diana Lamplugh, twenty-four when her second child was born, was both personally and socially forceful; her father's sister, who married a rear-admiral and was a woman of striking energy and authority, had been a female model in her life. But Diana Lamplugh lacked a higher education, a career or a cause. She was seriously overweight, and suffered from stress. She loved her children but hated housework and longed to return to her old job at the BBC. Then, during the years when Susannah was learning to walk and speak, she finally found just such a cause for herself. Her life soon began to change.

With a friend she founded Slimnastics – a 'method of fitness and relaxation' involving a 'positive approach to health through exercise, sensible eating, preventive medicine and tension control'. She said later that Slimnastics not only helped her lose weight but made her more stable and happy, and helped keep her sane. Her involvement meant setting up groups around the country and giving talks to them about the need for fitness, exercise, and careful eating habits. Later she would even co-author books on the subject and occasionally appear on television.

The headquarters for Slimnastics became the Lamplugh family household – the semi-detached house in Mortlake to which parents and children moved when Susannah was four. It was in East Sheen Avenue, a short walk from Richmond Park and Roehampton golf course and an exclusively white middle-class suburban milieu from where solicitors, civil servants and bank managers commuted daily into central London. It was an area which traditionally returned Liberal councillors and the Lamplughs were among those who voted Liberal – although they remained strong supporters of Margaret Thatcher and her Conservative government. There was an Anglican church half-way up the road, where Susannah became a chorister and her father a churchwarden.

By the standards of some of their neighbours, the Lamplughs were by no means wealthy. They relied on Paul Lamplugh's salary as a junior solicitor, working mainly on conveyancing for a Lincoln's Inn firm. For many years they also took in student lodgers, which supplemented the fees from Diana Lamplugh's swimming and Slimnastics classes. Lamplugh himself made a mid-career change when Susannah was eight, leaving law practice to become an administrator at the Law Society.

It was clear when the children went to school, however, that something was wrong. Susannah was not doing well academically, and soon fell seriously behind in reading and writing. Richard fared even worse, and both suffered (and continued to suffer) from the stigma of being considered well below average scholastically. In some desperation Susannah's parents took her out of the state Heathmere primary school when she was ten, and put her in a new co-educational private school run in a large Victorian house overlooking Kew Gardens and called the Unicorn School. By the time she was eleven, Susannah was diagnosed as suffering from dyslexia – a reading and writing disability sometimes attributed to mental or emotional problems but more usually to a neurological disorder.

It meant that school work for her was exacting and often confusing, for she found it very hard to read or write down what she heard. She had difficulty distinguishing between certain letters and syllables, and became nervous when asked to read out loud – which only increased her anxiety. Between hearing a word and writing it down, the letters would become scrambled. She would write 'travel' when she meant 'trail', 'untied' for 'undid', and confuse Bs and Ps. She could not easily make logical deductions either, and in history lessons would sometimes recount historical events in the wrong order. Her condition required patient, dedicated teaching.

But despite the handicap her remedial teacher found her to be a 'delightful friendly girl', with a satisfactory intelligence quotient of around 120. Her spelling was always to remain poor in the same way that her mother's had – as an adult Susannah would 'descide' to have a 'harty' breakfast – but she was able to continue a normal education. From Unicorn she was sent across the river to the Godolphin and Latymer School, a girls' school founded in 1905. Because of her disability she tended to be always a year behind the other girls, which she hated. Her school reports stressed the need for hard work if she was to make academic progress, and her parents sent her to private tutors.

Examinations would literally make her ill: she became extremely nervous, suffering from stomach cramps or complaints like shingles. But her father helped her, poring patiently over her school books with her every night. She subsequently passed six O-levels – English Literature, Geography, Biology, Mathematics, Scripture and Domestic Science. Then she transferred to Kingston College, where she failed to gain an A-level in English Literature but passed Biology – again with her father's help. In her teenage years she worked hard in the evenings and at weekends: as a waitress at the Bank of England Sports Ground, at the local delicatessen (where great dramas were once caused when she accidently sliced her thumb).

She grew up an obliging child, always keen to do right and please her mother. Diana Lamplugh sometimes found her eldest daughter taking care of *her*: ironing her clothes, sewing on buttons, advising on make-up. She was good-mannered, well dressed, invariably a credit to her parents – and popular with her peers too. She also shared much of the ambition, drive and attitudes of her family. Her appearance was important to her, and she plucked her eyebrows dramatically when she was twelve because she was already concerned with how she looked. She became a Queen's Guide at the local church. Her mother, with Slimnastics now in full swing, was particularly enthusiastic about swimming – and night after night the teenage Susannah would insist on training at the Putney Ladies' Swimming Club, swimming dozens of lengths at a time with strenuous physical exercises between each length.

Even in early adolescence, while her younger sister Tamsin was rebelling spectacularly, Susannah tended to be the good, exemplary daughter – always clearing up after her without having to be told, bubbling and chirpy at her parents' East Sheen Avenue parties, mothering her youngest sister Elizabeth into the ways of rectitude and obedience. In the words of a family friend, she was her mother's 'star pupil'. She became interested in Slimnastics and even qualified as a 'leader'. She naturally became the organizer of the family: when it came to her parents' anniversaries, she would be the one who would supervise the family gifts. For Paul and Diana Lamplugh's Silver Wedding, she arranged that they should receive a silver bottle-cooler from their children. For her parents' birthdays she would buy generous and carefully chosen presents: ornamental stone lions for the garden for her mother, binoculars for her father. Sometimes she would organize surprise visits to the cinema or theatre for them, asking them to keep their diaries free and then presenting them with tickets she had bought. She kept illustrated diaries of family holidays, and made cakes and Christmas puddings for the family – always with great energy and enthusiasm. But she also felt under strain, worrying a great deal too. She was a perfectionist in much of what she did. Family gatherings, such as at Christmas, would often give her stomach trouble.

Holidays were invariably spent in Wales, where Diana Lamplugh – with other members of her family – had been left a large house on the coast near Newport. The Lamplugh children were encouraged to bring friends, and dormitories for boys and girls were established in the attic. Meals would be cheerfully cooked for thirty at a time by Diana Lamplugh, and there would be windsurfing, sailing, all manner of fun; it involved stupendous feats of organization. The children's friends became the parents' friends too. The accent would always be on activities. Everybody would pitch in.

Back at home, Diana Lamplugh started writing long letters to her son at boarding school, minutely detailing her activities and those of her other children. Copies of the letters would then be filed and circulated to relatives by her husband. The daily doings of the Lamplughs, seen through Diana Lamplugh's eyes, were thus recorded. The letters pulsated with enthusiasm, and few domestic details were too trivial to escape them. 'Mrs Whyte and I have just mended a fuse on the Hoover,' recounted one. The Welsh holidays were also a subject that came under close scrutiny: 'We did such a lot what with fishing, sailing, canoeing, just charging around in the boat, swimming (so often), mending the engines, digging out the patio, playing tennis, shooting, riding, flying the glider, climbing the mountain, mob-mob [*sic*], Grandpop's birthday party, the picnic at the farm, the evening visit to Llyngwyair by the boats, all those many visits to the pubs by your gang, Uncle Hugh buying the girls drinks in the club and so on and so on . . .' There was frequent family advice too: 'Don't forget that I judge our students' parents by the way they behave – so you mustn't let us down.' The letters became a long-standing family joke to Susannah and her brother and sisters. She lightheartedly complained that they were boring, far too detailed, and were not even always read.

By the time she was sixteen Susannah had met her first serious boyfriend. His name was Barry Steele – known as 'Baz' – and he was two years older than her. They met at the Bull disco in Sheen, and soon became inseparable. There were quarrels with her parents about how late she could stay out, and on one occasion she did not return until 12.45 a.m. Steele bought a car, and the two went for long drives into the countryside. They seemed to friends to be almost like a middle-aged couple, stolid and secure and even unadventurous in their relationship. But she loved him: as Diana Lamplugh drove along Upper Richmond Road one day, she saw the young couple arm in arm, twirling around and around in ever-faster circles, happy and laughing. But it was not as simple as that. Baz was a butcher's boy, and the son of a butcher. Though the Lamplughs liked him he did not blend in well with the social aspirations and ethos of East Sheen Avenue. To Paul Lamplugh he was 'a typical butcher's boy, no more than that'. To Diana Lamplugh, Baz was not a suitable boyfriend or potential husband for her daughter. He even smelled of meat, she thought. He did not wash as often as she would like. He failed to rise from his chair when she came into the room. Even Leo, the faithful family retriever, did not seem to like him. And with all the late nights the relationship was threatening to interfere with Susannah's school work too.

It caused some alarm in the household when Baz first asked Susannah to go away on holiday with him. Her father, in particular, was very opposed to the idea: his daughter was still only sixteen. But finally he and his wife relented, allowing the pair not only to go camping together in their Volkswagen van but also to holiday in Spain with Baz's family. But it was not long before Diana Lamplugh hit on a solution to the Baz problem. She would send Susannah to the United States to stay with the family of one of her American student lodgers and that of her brother Mark in Vermont. The hope was that faced with new transatlantic vistas, Susannah would forget about Baz and see more of life.

But Susannah herself did not want to go, and missed her flight from Heathrow after being delayed in the ladies' toilet with stomach trouble. By the time she went to the departure gate, it was too late. Despite ticket problems, however, her mother managed to get her on a flight the following day. Five weeks later seventeen-year-old Susannah returned tanned and with an 'I Love New York' T-shirt, speaking of her adventures on Greyhound buses and in Manhattan – and three new boyfriends. 'It all worked just as well and even better than I had hoped,' her mother confided to a family newsletter that then did the rounds. Baz, the now heartbroken butcher's boy, was on the way out of Susannah Lamplugh's life. 'Poor old Baz has finally seemed to take the message,' confirmed Diana Lamplugh in a subsequent circulated letter, 'though he sent some beautiful flowers that must have cost the earth.'

For Susannah, finding the right man would increasingly become a preoccupation. Should she, for example, marry for love or money? It would prove a dilemma, but her thoughts were also turning now to a career. She was nineteen and attracted to the bright lights and a life of money and glitz and action; ideally her job would provide a path to a more affluent and exciting life where she would meet interesting people. Her dyslexia was a drawback in whatever career she was to follow, and Diana Lamplugh gave her some advice: 'If you're dyslexic you have to *be* somebody, rather than *do* something.' Her mother suggested that she became an air hostess, but finally Susannah decided to be a beautician. She duly applied to become a student at Joan Price's Face Place, a fashionable ladies' make-up establishment started in Chelsea thirteen years before by a fashion journalist. The course lasted a year, and led to a diploma from the Confederation of Beauty Therapy and Cosmetology (and its European equivalent), involving courses in anatomy, physiology, chemistry and home economics, as well as practical training.

Again Susannah applied herself with perfectionist zeal, and again Paul Lamplugh coached her through her written work. The course cost over £2,000 and she attended from 9.30 to

4.00 each day – practising beauty treatments on other young women students. Her sister Tamsin frequently found herself drafted in to be a model for facials, electrolysis and similar work. The owner, Joan Constantinidi (née Price), believed her to be an ideal pupil – popular, cheerful and with an essential streak of naïvety. She was a *caring* person, who thought the best of people and worked well with colleagues; she would have made a good nurse, Constantinidi thought. When Susannah qualified at twenty, she was immediately offered a job in the Face Place salon as a qualified beautician. With tips she would make more than £100 a week, working from 10 a.m. to 6 p.m. and the occasional Saturday – and most clients thought she was extremely good at her job.

But it was hard work, and gradually Susannah realized that beauty work such as this was taking her nowhere. It involved long hours, with rich women pouring out their problems to her whether she liked it or not. It was physically tiring too, and she did not make a lot of money even with tips. But she did have the opportunity to meet people like Pamela Spurr-Seager at Joan Price's, and sometimes could do private beauty work in her clients' homes. It was the kind of work she could do anywhere too, possibly even abroad. She was able to moonlight at a shop called Secrets in Barnes, and at other places. She had already gained experience as an Avon lady selling cosmetics door-to-door in the evenings. By working so hard, she was already showing an ability that would stagger future boyfriends. Though she earned comparatively little, she was especially good at managing money and was organized, methodical and sparing with it. Friends wondered how she managed to save money so easily, and predicted that one day she would be rich.

By now she was also living away from home. The clashes between the volatile Tamsin and her mother had grown in intensity; her disc jockey boyfriend did not meet with Diana Lamplugh's approval either. Finally the position in East Sheen Avenue became so overwrought that Diana decided her second daughter would have to move out – and that Susannah, with whom she had a much better relationship, should accompany her. She went through the house collecting all Tamsin's belongings in preparation for the move, and when Tamsin returned home and saw what had happened she was livid. But Susannah was happier with the idea, and she and her mother soon found a small two-bedroomed house to rent in Walham Grove, close to Fulham police station. The rent was to be split three ways, between Susannah, Tamsin and their mother.

Before long both sisters felt happier for the move. They began to value their independence, and found Fulham more invigorating than Mortlake. Each began to gain in confidence. But for a young London woman of nineteen, Susannah was still surprisingly naïve. She had lived her life as a model daughter and her work involved a restricted, women-only life. She seemed 'prim and proper' – conservatively and impeccably dressed, polite and well-spoken, her middle-class suburban tones tinged with just a suggestion of south London. There seemed to be a streak of puritanism within her, and the ill-fated relationship with Baz had been the only serious relationship she had ever had. Her parents felt that she should have had more boyfriends by now.

It was not long before her life began to move in that direction. By now she was twenty and earning a salary at Joan Price's Face Place, living away from home and less under the influence of her mother. But family holidays in Wales were still *de rigueur*, and that summer she met the man who was to be the most enduring boyfriend of her life until her disappearance. Dave Hodgkinson was twenty-three and – to Susannah – tall, bronzed

67

and very handsome. His official occupation was carpenter, but his father was a retired Indian Army officer and he had been to public school at Eastbourne. He was an enthusiastic windsurfer, and was quietly spoken and intense. He had originally been invited to Wales through his friends Mike Hough and Doug Williams.

To Hodgkinson the coast around Newport seemed romantic, with the halyards clinking in the estuary at night. He was bowled over by Susannah when he first saw her, and liked Tamsin too. The elder of the two sisters had the ability, he thought, to *light up* a group of people, and was very beautiful. It was difficult to establish any kind of rapport with her in the wholesome atmosphere of separate dormitories in the Lamplugh household – couples were not encouraged to go off on their own – but after four days he asked Susannah to go for a walk with him, despite the embarrassment of revealing his keenness in front of the others.

It was the start of an enduring relationship. It continued in London, where Hodgkinson took her to see his favourite films like *Young Frankenstein*. He visited the Lamplugh sisters regularly at Walham Grove, and at first neither Tamsin nor Susannah was sure which of the two interested him. It took them several weeks to find out, after a group of young men and women borrowed Paul and Diana Lamplugh's van to go to the Wales house for the weekend. Without the parents, the notion of separate dormitories held less fast. The morning after their arrival Tamsin burst into her sister's bedroom, and found her in bed with Hodgkinson. To their relief, Tamsin smiled and came in to sit on the bed with them. All was well.

Back in London the relationship thrived and Susannah started to become more worldly. Initially Hodgkinson found her sheltered and inexperienced, both professionally and sexually.

68

Her life, he thought, tended to be unusually compartmentalized. In Wales, for example, she would be much more relaxed and would somehow look more attractive than she did in London – where her manner would be more formal. He also found her unusually secretive, but when they were close she soon started to confide in him. They started to see each other six nights a week, and Hodgkinson called in to the house in Walham Grove every time he passed on his motorcycle. She called him 'Hodge' or 'Splodge', and he would refer to her affectionately as 'Suze', or 'Pratt' or 'Biffo'. Susannah particularly admired his mother, a successful career woman who nevertheless baked cakes and darned socks and happily fulfilled her image of motherhood. 'A *real* mother,' she would say. Her own mother admitted she was not a natural housekeeper.

She celebrated her twenty-first birthday with her family in Wales, though once again was struck by nervous stomach trouble as the time for her party drew near. She spent much of the time ill in bed. Socially, she entered new circles in London with Dave Hodgkinson, because the relationship also meant Susannah's active involvement in the Putney Set. Hough, who had shared a flat with Hodgkinson, bought a flat in Putney – and with Doug Williams they formed the core of a group that met regularly in the pubs and wine bars of Putney and Fulham and discussed their careers and ambitions, windsurfing and other pastimes. Tamsin, Susannah's sister, also became a member. It was a group vaguely similar to what had come to be known in socially aspiring London circles as 'Sloanes', and Susannah Lamplugh's increasing resemblance to a so-called Sloane was by now firmly in train.

The trouble was that being a beautician was not an occupation suitable for a Sloane, or even for a member of the Putney Set.

If Susannah could acquire her own business – and Spurr-Seager had indeed suggested that one day the two of them could establish their own beauty and fitness centre – that would be different. But in the meantime Susannah had been nurturing a new ambition, one that *would* impress the Putney Set and yet enable her to remain a beautician. If she left Joan Price's Face Place to work for a Steiner Hair and Beauty Centre – Mr Steiner had been a fashionable London hairdresser – she might find a route towards a more stimulating way of life, for the Steiner group had a contract with Cunard to provide and run the beauty salons on their ships. Her mother's younger brother Mike worked in the hotel business and offered to help with contacts – and almost immediately Susannah landed a job as a beautician on the *QE2*.

Sailing away on the majestic liner was to prove the turning point in Susannah Lamplugh's life. Her brother and sisters each went away to boarding school, but Susannah had always lived in the orbit of East Sheen Avenue. Now she would be away living below decks on what amounted to a permanent cruise, one of the few young women among a vast complement of men on the ship. She would shuttle between New York and Southampton – and later in the year, she hoped, she would be invited on to the 'Worldy', the prized world cruise. She was twenty-two when she first sailed down the Solent, heading for a new life of independence and freedom. Where boyfriends were concerned, she would now make up for lost time. Her prim and proper exterior would remain, but that streak of puritanism would fade away.

For the detectives, all this was highly relevant. Whether anyone liked it or not, Susannah Lamplugh's personal life was now crucial to this inquiry. A former boyfriend or jealous contact, after all, might well hold the key to her disappearance

– and all such people would have to be located, investigated and eliminated. A major task that now awaited the police, for example, was to talk in depth to members of the Putney Set, in the hope that someone there could provide some clues about Susannah's life. It would prove a peculiarly difficult and sometimes exasperating experience for them, because so few would prove able to come up with any useful information.

The police's reconstruction of events on the last Monday of July, meanwhile, was bringing forth literally hundreds of new witnesses. Two men in particular – Noel Devere, a thirty-year-old unemployed bar-cellar man, and Nicholas Doyle, forty-one, an unemployed jeweller – would each come forward to tell police that they had definitely seen Susannah outside 37 Shorrolds Road that lunchtime. Doyle would tell them that he had seen a man with her too, and would give detectives the best description of a man yet – better even than Riglin's.

But where did this leave Wendy Jones's insistence that Susannah's car was parked in Stevenage Road at the time the two men had supposedly seen her in Shorrolds Road, over a mile away? Or Barbara Whitfield's equally adamant sighting of her friend Susannah in her white Ford Fiesta later that afternoon? What about the Putney Set? Why had no one who had seen Susannah leave her Sturgis office come forward? The questions were proliferating all the time – but the answers, it seemed, were becoming increasingly elusive.

Chapter Six

That Sunday, the first since Susannah's disappearance, the Lamplughs went to church. It was another warm summer's day, the sun streaming in through the stained-glass windows above the altar. Less than a decade before, Susannah had sung at this very same church, wearing her red cassock and white ruff just like the other choirboys and girls. The church choir was still there, but now Susannah was gone. For Paul and Diana Lamplugh there was a sudden full realization of what had happened when the vicar held a minute's silence for their daughter. There was total silence – no journalists, no police, no fussing neighbours to direct them and their thoughts away from awful reality. The full pain and sorrow, the undiluted and unbearable truth, pierced into their consciousness at precisely this time.

But as they were leaving the church, Diana Lamplugh spotted Dr Desmond Kelly in the departing congregation. She was reluctant to ask his advice, for she was certain in her mind that she did not herself need any kind of psychiatric help or guidance. But she was worried about her husband, she explained later, because his interview at the Law Society was now imminent. In some ways, too, he seemed to have taken Susannah's disappearance harder than her. He could not cope, for example, with gruesome speculation about what might have happened to their daughter. So she asked Kelly for his advice. 'Keep busy,' came his reply. 'Keep so busy you sleep from tiredness. You must not dwell on the pain and futility of it all.' It was advice that Diana Lamplugh was to take to heart in the coming months. She walked home with her husband and their first project was to clear out their garage, heaving out old possessions with great enthusiasm.

By this time, their son Richard had finally come home, although their two daughters, Tamsin and Elizabeth, were still in New Zealand. For a week Richard had been living on his own at the Hertfordshire fish farm, unable to bring himself to discuss his sister's disappearance with his parents. He could not stop thinking of Susannah, and had only the fish and the skies for company. But Doug Williams had volunteered with another friend to spend the night with him, and that eased his loneliness. Home in London Richard joined the therapeutic garage clear-out, and when he returned to work after the weekend he felt more able to discuss what had happened to his sister.

Then Diana Lamplugh threw herself into a new project, the redecoration and conversion of part of the house. It had been planned long before Susannah's disappearance. She supervised volunteers as they cleared her office and rearranged files, went through her medicines, pruned the roses, boiled all the tea towels, made her collection of hats more orderly, tidied the kitchen cupboards. All was hustle and bustle in the Lamplugh household, and the builders soon started work. In the coming weeks such activity around her would help Diana Lamplugh cope with what she called 'the horrors' – sudden vivid images of what could have happened to her daughter.

But what *had* happened? By the end of the second week, the trail had gone alarmingly cold. There was no sign of Susannah, no forensic evidence to suggest where she had gone after leaving her office, no witnesses who had come forward having seen any abduction or fight or even argument – and no obvious suspect. (The taxi fare who was supposed to have seen a couple having a fight never materialized.) There was not even the slightest evidence to suggest a crime had been committed.

Few, if any missing persons inquiries, the detectives were now feeling, had ever been so mystifying or so devoid of helpful information. The Lamplugh squad was meeting every morning and afternoon at its Kensington headquarters to discuss new developments, theories and possibilities: Detective Superintendent Carter believed in a democratic approach to major investigations, letting even the most junior policeman or woman in the team have his or her say. But what Doyle and Devere and all the other witnesses from the Shorrolds Road area were now telling them only strengthened their original theory – that Susannah must have got into a car belonging to someone she trusted. It seemed inconceivable that she could have been abducted in broad daylight from a busy London street without *someone* hearing or seeing something. But apparently no one had, despite strenuous efforts to find anyone.

It still did not make sense to them that Susannah's car was in Stevenage Road at around 12.45 – while she herself was supposedly in Shorrolds Road at the same time. Devere, the unemployed barman, was specific about *his* timings because he had just come from collecting his unemployment benefit, and was in a hurry to meet his wife at 1.30. He remembered that as he walked into Shorrolds Road, he glanced at his watch and saw it was 12.50. Then he came to the house with a Sturgis 'For Sale' sign outside, which he noticed because he particularly liked the house. He saw a young woman clutching a set of keys in her right hand, standing on her own in the gateway of number 37 and looking out towards the street. He did not take much notice of her because he was in a hurry, but having seen all the publicity about the case he was now in little doubt that the woman was Susannah Lamplugh.

Equally certain that he had seen Susannah was Doyle, the unemployed jeweller. Like Harry Riglin he remembered a man with her too, but could not be specific about times – only that it was sometime between midday and four o'clock. The woman was standing on the pavement looking up at number 37, he recalled, and he thought at the time that she and the man a few paces away both looked too smart to be interested in this particular £128,000 house. The man was between twenty-five and thirty, with dark swept-back hair and wearing an 'immaculate and expensive' charcoal grey suit. His nose looked as though it might have been broken at some time, Doyle thought. Perhaps he was an ex-serviceman or a former public schoolboy who had been injured playing rugby, he suggested – or, alternatively, a very well-dressed East End villain.

Three other witnesses had by now given interesting evidence too. Jesus Inchusta, a thirty-year-old Spanish history teacher and tourist visiting London, told police he saw a young woman actually meeting a man outside the house in Shorrolds Road. He said he noticed the girl because she was smiling, and he gave a description that fitted Susannah's. The man who met her, he went on, was between twenty-six and thirty-two, tall, good-looking, slender – and so well dressed he could have been a male fashion model. But Mr Inchusta was worried that the artist's impression of the man that had been in the newspapers – the one drawn by a Putney artist, and based on Riglin's evidence - was not very accurate. He thought the man's hair was longer and his face thinner.

Then Mrs Elizabeth Hammond, a seventy-one-year-old pensioner, came forward to say that she had parked her red Volvo in Shorrolds Road that day, and returned at 1.10 to see a large dark saloon car with two men sitting in it. They were not speaking and were just looking ahead of them, motionless.

The driver was in his thirties, and had black hair, a moustache and was of medium build. He was wearing a dark suit. And Marianna Jagoda, a thirty-seven-year-old waitress who lived in Stevenage Road, reported seeing a young woman standing outside a house in her road that had a Sturgis 'For Sale' sign outside it. She was on her own, carrying papers or books, and she had formed the impression the woman was waiting for someone. Then she saw a man with a dark briefcase, aged between forty and fifty, with a 'good suntan' and dark brown hair. Had Susannah possibly shown 'Mr Kipper' a house in Stevenage Road after they left Shorrolds Road?

Doyle and Devere each added a point that gave their evidence added plausibility. The girl they had seen, they told the police, had lighter hair than the pictures of Susannah showed. This fascinated the detectives, because in the meantime they had discovered that Susannah had been to have her hair highlighted at Studio 213 in Fulham Road on the Friday before she disappeared. There she had paid a hairdresser named Marc Jacobs £18.50 for a haircut and highlights. The pictures of her published across the country were not, therefore, exact likenesses. By the time she disappeared, her hair was lighter and cut differently from that of the Suzy the nation had come to know. Doyle also added an important detail. He thought the man he had seen was holding a champagne bottle with a red, white and blue ribbon around its neck.

That was another intriguing piece of information for the detectives, because it gave a clue to the type of man they might be looking for: someone with an expensive lifestyle, a flashy dresser who possibly wanted to impress the attractive young woman from Sturgis. The wedding of the Duke and Duchess of York had been just five days before, and local branches of Peter Dominic, a wine and spirits chain, were selling decorated champagne bottles as a special promotion – so it seemed quite possible that what Doyle had told them was correct. Police scoured all the shops selling such champagne bottles, but no one remembered any customer fitting the descriptions. Had the man invited Susannah somewhere to drink the champagne with him, perhaps after they had looked over the house? If so, where? For two days Special Patrol Group officers had visited every type of wine bar, restaurant and pub in the area, but still could find no one who had seen a couple matching the descriptions.

By now the media coverage seemed unquenchable. More witnesses were coming forward all the time as a result, though they rarely had any useful information. But Richard Turner, a thirty-year-old businessman and car enthusiast, was an exception. He told the detectives that he had driven up Shorrolds Road between 12.30 and 1.00 p.m. the day Susannah went missing. Cars were parked both sides of the road, he said, but he remembered in particular three cars that were double-parked. One was a white Ford Fiesta and another a navy blue BMW. It was a model from the early to mid-1970s, he thought, one similar to a BMW 518 with four doors. It was parked almost outside number 37. And some way behind it was *another* white Ford Fiesta, possibly with someone sitting in it.

Turner was reliable, the detectives decided, and his special knowledge of cars gave his evidence added authority. The older BMWs were distinctive and relatively unusual cars, and if 'Mr Kipper' owned or drove one the information could narrow the field of suspects down considerably. Turner's sighting of a white Ford Fiesta, too, suggested that Susannah had indeed driven to Shorrolds Road to show number 37 to 'Mr Kipper'. But why was her car found in Stevenage Road? And why were there *two* white Ford Fiestas in Shorrolds Road?

If the man she met that day was someone she knew – a client or perhaps a jilted lover, say – the next logical step for the police team was to trace all Susannah's male friends and contacts. They would then have to ask them to account for their movements on that day, and eliminate them one by one – now making a special point of finding out if they had access to dark-coloured BMWs. Leegood had already been through the treatment, and was now totally clear of suspicion. Though Hodgkinson's exact movements on his way home from Corsica were impossible to verify, the detectives were now satisfied he was not involved in any way. Hough was also formally cleared. By all accounts Mark Gurdon, the manager of the Sturgis office, did not have any romantic or sexual entanglement with Susannah – but as someone close to her professionally he too had to be investigated. That lunchtime, he told police, he was in the Crocodile Tears wine bar – a stone's throw from the office – with colleagues from other Sturgis offices. The colleagues duly confirmed his story.

Detectives knew already that Susannah wanted to end her relationship with Leegood, because she had discussed doing so with several friends and colleagues. They had established, too, that Leegood was away in the Canary Islands for a week until four days before Susannah disappeared. Did this mean that she had met someone else in the meantime? The story of her romantic life was already complex enough, for Susannah lived life at a furious pace. Even by Day Two, police had found a twenty-five-year-old man who told them he had a sexual relationship with her during the months before her disappearance – and who happened to live in Shorrolds Road itself, only a matter of yards from number 37. But that turned out to be pure coincidence, and he was quickly cleared. There were at least two other men with whom Susannah had been similarly close in the month before her disappearance, so besides their profile of her life and character police started to trace in detail her movements for the ten days or so immediately before her disappearance.

What interested them in particular was a party Susannah attended on the Saturday night before. Might she have met 'Mr Kipper' there? It was a typical Putney Set affair, held in a barn and marquee in the garden of a house in Capel, Dorking, Surrey – prime suburban commuter territory twenty-three miles south of London. The party was to celebrate the twenty-first birthday of Siobhan Grinling – also an estate agent and a member of the Set - and was held at her parents' home. There were more than seventy young men and women there, nearly all of them in their twenties, and Susannah wore a peach dress she had made herself. Everyone sat in a man/woman/man formation for dinner, and had to change places between courses. Drink flowed freely. A cabaret with a female limbo dancer was followed by a disco, and the party did not end until 3.00 a.m.

That night Susannah stayed at the home of Michael and Sarah Hough's parents in Ockley, ten minutes' drive from the party. She had been picked up at her flat in Disraeli Road by Sarah Hough, and they arrived in Ockley about 6.00 p.m. They changed and had a few drinks, then went on to the party at about 8.30. Nothing unusual happened there, and Susannah was not seen to dance with anyone who was not known to the Set. She looked particularly resplendent in her new dress, friends reported. But during the meal she did let slip some information which was possibly significant. She was working on a deal, she confided to a fellow guest, that if successful would mean she was due for a large commission – possibly as much as £3,000. She was also hopeful that she would soon be buying a property in a joint deal with someone, she added. She talked about two unsuccessful attempts to sell her flat, and how she hoped to clinch a sale soon. But that was all. No one could remember her talking about which property was involved, or which clients, or which friends or associates. Were these some freelance projects of her own that Sturgis knew nothing about? Who were the mystery people?

Next morning everyone got up around ten o'clock, leaving the Houghs' house two hours later for an afternoon's windsurfing at Worthing. Susannah and Sarah Hough loaded their surfboards on to Hough's car, and with a twenty-nine-year-old market researcher named Andrew Black, they arrived at the coast at about two in the afternoon. Leegood, who was just back from his holiday, had not been to the party but joined the windsurfing on the Sunday afternoon. Susannah excelled at the solitary sport of windsurfing, skimming over the waves for hours with effortless control and precision. The group broke up at 5.30, with Susannah and Black returning in Hough's car, Leegood making his own way back to London. Back in Putney Susannah took her surfboard up to her flat, then drove in her office car to see her parents in East Sheen Avenue. It was a characteristically hectic weekend for her, and even she felt tired.

She wanted to see her parents because it was her mother's fiftieth birthday on the following Wednesday, and she had already explained to Diana Lamplugh that she could not come to a birthday lunch that day because she would not be able to get the time off work. Sturgis were apparently strict about that sort of thing. But with her brother and sisters she had organized a pre-birthday weekend treat for both parents: a stay at Le Meridien Hotel in Piccadilly (which Tamsin, working for the hotel agency, had arranged from New Zealand), flowers, champagne and a trip to the theatre to see *La Cage aux Folles*.

Susannah had left them a note: 'Here are some theatre tickets. The performance starts at 8. There is some champagne in the fridge to start off the evening. I hope you enjoy yourselves. Lots of love.' She wanted to know all about the birthday treat and how it had gone, and also took the opportunity to bring some dirty washing home. Paul and Diana Lamplugh told her about their weekend treat, and she described the party. They kissed goodbye at about 9 p.m. and then she drove off in her white Ford Fiesta. That was the last time Diana and Paul Lamplugh saw her.

She apparently went straight home to Disraeli Road. That evening she had an arrangement with Leegood that he would join her at her flat if they were in London before eight o'clock, but Leegood was delayed returning from Worthing. They spoke on the phone later that evening, however, and discussed the arrangements for a party the following Tuesday. It was to be at the flat of a wealthy young man who lived in Park Lane, in the heart of Mayfair – a friend of Leegood whom Susannah had come to know well while Leegood was in the Canary Islands earlier in the month.

That was the kind of information the detectives needed. Had Susannah developed a secret relationship with this man while Leegood was away and shortly before she disappeared? It turned out that she had originally met the man at a ball earlier in the month given by the Honourable Artillery Company, of which both Leegood and Doug Williams were part-time territorial members. The man lived much of the year in the Bahamas (where Leegood had first met him) but now divided his time between the Caribbean and Britain. A fortnight after meeting him, it turned out, Susannah had gone alone to the man's flat for a Saturday night party – and then accompanied him to Club 151 in King's Road. There she also danced with a stockbroker who had apparently been fined for insider dealing. (Police finally traced this mystery man through the American Express card slip he had used to pay for champagne at the club, and were then able to rule him out of their inquiries.) Then the wealthy young man from the Bahamas and Susannah went on to the Garden Club in Kensington. He later insisted (according to the Bahamas police after they interviewed him) that he and Susannah subsequently caught separate taxis home at 2 a.m.

But he did not deny that Susannah was in his flat in Park Lane when friends came round at 10.00 the following morning. The reason she was there then, he went on to explain, was that she returned to the flat early on the Sunday morning to see with him the televised recording of a boxing match. She then watched the boxing, in which Tim Witherspoon of the United States defeated Frank Bruno of Britain. But Susannah herself had a slightly different version of the weekend's events. 'Guess where I spent Saturday night!' she exclaimed to colleagues at Sturgis the following Monday morning. There was still some distance to travel, socially and economically, between Putney and Park Lane – but Susannah Lamplugh was getting there.

Could this flurry of excitement in her life, shortly before she disappeared, be crucial to the inquiry? The wealthy young man's movements for the day – and those of other people she had met at his party – would now have to be carefully scrutinized by detectives. But otherwise the weekend before the Monday seemed to yield little useful information. The phone call with Leegood was at about 10.15 on the Sunday evening, and that was the last he spoke to her. Next morning Susannah's flatmate Nick Bryant left for work at around 7.45. Susannah was still in the flat, wearing a white dressing gown. Then (it was assumed) she had breakfast, walked from her flat to her car, and joined all the other commuters for the drive across the Thames to work. And Susannah Lamplugh's last morning at work, routine and unremarkable, duly began.

The possibility that Susannah had deliberately gone missing was by now looking less and less likely. She clearly did not have any money worries, although detectives were still mystified as to how she managed to maintain such a relatively expensive lifestyle. She did not appear to have any great personal worries either, and although she had many boyfriends she seemed to be able to remain on good terms with them afterwards. Exceptionally, police could find no known enemies of Susannah Lamplugh. She had left her handbag, with lipstick and other personal articles, beside her desk when she left her office. Even her purse, with £15 inside, was left in her car. Her flat, which she was hoping to sell for £73,950, remained unsold. She had been making plans for the following week, too. She intended to pick up her missing cheque book that Monday evening, have lunch with Pamela Spurr-Seager on the Tuesday and go to the plush Park Lane party on Tuesday evening. She was also going to watch an American football match at Wembley the following Saturday. Everybody reported that she had acted completely normally at the Saturday night party and in the other days leading up to her appointment with 'Mr Kipper'. If she had deliberately staged her disappearance, she had done so exceedingly cleverly and thoroughly.

But there was still a glimmer of hope that she was alive, if only because there was no proof that she was dead. In New Zealand, Tamsin and Elizabeth Lamplugh had still not really taken in what was happening on the other side of the world. From the remote camp site Tamsin had spoken to Diana Lamplugh on her fiftieth birthday, but because she knew her mother was so prone to dramatization she and her sister had failed to grasp the gravity of what had happened. Diana Lamplugh had in any case played it down in order not to upset her two daughters unnecessarily. Tamsin still panicked nevertheless and felt bereft at the thought that her sister was gone, but was calmed down by Elizabeth. They went back to finish a meal they had started at their camp site. Ironically, Susannah had been envious of Elizabeth's trip: she had wanted to go herself, but decided it would be too expensive. With characteristic resourcefulness she had even explored the possibility of obtaining her passage as an air courier. But it did not work out and now Tamsin and Elizabeth were camping in the mild winter of New Zealand, and their sister was missing in the midst of a faraway English summer.

They soon decided to drive south to Auckland, where Tamsin had a flat. But, frustratingly, it was without a phone to keep in touch with England, and they had to rely on a nearby callbox. Tamsin returned to work in Auckland exactly a week after Susannah had gone missing – while her sister stayed at home, watching videos during the day. Both had convinced themselves that whatever had happened to Susannah was only a temporary problem: it was bound to be resolved. Elizabeth, with all the cheeerful nonchalance of youth, continued the holiday her parents had given her as a reward for passing O-levels, by flying to Hong Kong as though nothing had happened.

But within a week, Tamsin realized that she could not bear the isolation of being so far from home. She was also potentially a major help to the police, because few knew Susannah better than she did. Besides being her sister, she was perhaps Susannah's closest female friend and could know vital facts about Susannah which no one else knew. From Kensington a senior detective spoke to her on the phone in New Zealand, and established that she would bring home any letters she might have received from Susannah. Private sister-to-sister letters, he hoped, might contain vital clues about any recent developments in what Susannah lightheartedly called the 'men field'.

Thirteen days after Susannah left her Sturgis office for the last time, her sister Tamsin boarded a British Airways flight in Auckland. Airline officials would not let her take her six suitcases without charging NZ$2,500 for excess baggage, so she arranged to send some of her cases by freight for NZ$250 instead. This meant, infuriatingly, that it would be another week before detectives could see the vital letters in London. For Tamsin there was then a thirty-hour flight, via Brisbane, Perth, Singapore and Bombay. She drank heavily on the plane, and two hours before arrival at Heathrow a stewardess suddenly asked her to move up to First Class, where she was served complimentary champagne. What she did not know was that Johnstone had arranged for her to be given VIP status at Heathrow, so police could move in to interview her as soon as the plane landed. She was taken to the door of the plane while it was still taxiing towards the terminal and was the first to leave the aircraft.

Her mother had warned her on the phone that there would be journalists and television crews waiting at Heathrow to interview her about her sister. That, once again, Tamsin thought, was her mother being dramatic. Of *course* no newspaper would be interested in her and her sister, even if Suze really was missing, she thought. She even became convinced on the flight that when she walked into the passenger area, Susannah would be there to meet her. But instead she was met at the plane by two plainclothes policemen, then taken in a daze to an office in Terminal Four. Detective Superintendent Carter and Detective Inspector Johnstone told her that they planned to drive her to Kensington immediately for debriefing. Customs men came to her and cleared what luggage she had. It was now Day Fourteen, and the story of missing estate agent Suzy Lamplugh was still front-page news across the nation. Journalists were speculating that perhaps Tamsin Lamplugh, aged twenty-four, could supply the clues to the mystery of what had happened to her sister.

But before she was driven to Kensington, Tamsin was allowed a few minutes with someone who had come to meet her. She was now in a bewildered haze, with the terrible realities of what was happening in London beginning to dawn on her. She was suffering both from the thirty-hour flight itself and the drinks she had taken during it. For the first time, she accepted that her sister really was missing, and maybe had gone for ever. Now she was going to be driven straight off into a strangely unfamiliar and forbidding world of plainclothes detectives and police incident rooms to try to help the police solve the mystery. In tears, she threw herself into the arms of her mother.

Chapter Seven

Before the end of the summer the investigation was concentrating more than ever on Susannah's private life. Because of her secretiveness, it was becoming both involved and time-consuming for the police. Tamsin, her sister, was unable to provide any crucial information about new boyfriends or contacts. The letters Susannah had written to her in New Zealand arrived in London a week after she flew into Heathrow, but despite careful scrutiny by detectives they produced no significant new clues either.

If Susannah had known her abductor and was possibly even involved in a property deal with him – as the detectives now thought likely possibilities – the logical deduction was that the man they were looking for featured somewhere in Susannah's past. A former client of Susannah's at Joan Price's Face Place recalled, for example, that about two years before her disappearance Susannah had mentioned having a relationship with a man whom the client thought may have been married. He lived in a luxurious flat in London, apparently, and cooked Susannah what she had said were splendid meals there. The client *thought* Susannah had told her the man went home at weekends to somewhere in the west country, possibly Bristol, and was about thirty-eight. But although she was desperately racking her brains, she could remember nothing more.

This mystery man, whoever he was, was unknown to either the Putney Set or to Diana and Paul Lamplugh. He had not come forward to be eliminated. Was this merely because he was married and reluctant to confess to an affair with another woman, or did he have something to hide? Was he possibly involved in setting up what the tabloid press called a 'love-nest' with Susannah? What was the mysterious business that kept him in London during the week and possibly in the West country at weekends? Did he, indeed, exist?

Every possible detail gleaned about the man was painstakingly cross-referenced in the police incident room, with each item, such as his age, marital status and where he lived separately indexed on cards. If there were any other apparently unconnected links with Bristol, say, the system would then bring them to light. Before long a list of all BMW owners in Bristol was compiled for police from the central computer licensing records, but there was absolutely no evidence that any of the hundreds of resulting names could be linked with Susannah Lamplugh in any way. It was becoming an all-too-familiar story: there was never enough *evidence*, and the police were in no position to accuse anyone of her abduction. Polite questioning about his movements on the day were as far as they could go with any possible suspect.

In the months following Susannah's disappearance there were many such separate inquiries, all of them pursued at the time with great enthusiasm. But the mystery man from Bristol, like some others in Susannah's life, was never traced. His name was not in any of her diaries or address books, and no friend knew anything definite about him. Diana Lamplugh was convinced he never existed. Her daughter would not have had the *time* to have a relationship with a married man, she insisted to friends.

What the episode showed, none the less, was the magnitude of the task ahead for the police. Inexorably the three years immediately before Susannah Lamplugh's disappearance – the first of them when she was sailing on the *QE*2, constantly meeting new people around the world – started to come under an intense spotlight, all in a concerted effort to uncover a suspect from her past. Some of the detectives were convinced that the name of the man they now so desperately wanted would already be in their massive card index system: it was a matter of putting the pieces of the jigsaw together. The hunt for Susannah Lamplugh had already become the most involved missing person inquiry in history.

Leaving her parents behind in London and sailing to New York when she was twenty-two, the detectives soon discovered, heralded the start of a decisive new phase in Susannah Lamplugh's young life. Before then she had no shortage of boyfriends, but despite this somehow remained prim and curiously unworldly. The experience of being at sea so long, living in closely confined crew quarters and visiting the most exotic resorts and cities of the world, rapidly changed all that. She became much more experimental sexually, almost as though she had suddenly discovered freedom and was now determined to exploit it. When she returned to London she drank more, and to the surprise of friends started to use swear words much more frequently. In the words of a close friend, working on the *QE*2 opened Susannah's eyes and mind to the world.

Several of the young women who had worked as beauticians on board the *QE*2 had in the past acquired a bad reputation. They were known to some of the crew as 'Steiner Tarts', and because men greatly outnumbered women in the ship's complement of around a thousand they were often sought after on the lower decks both socially and sexually. The white-coated women beauticians and the frequently homosexual male hairdressers made an exotic addition to the waiters, chefs and sailors on board the ship. But by the time Susannah first walked across the ship's gangway at Southampton, the position was already changing. This time, for example, the male hairdressers were not homosexual. There were twelve men and women in the Steiner enclave, comprising beauticians like Susannah, a chiropodist, men's barber and women's hair stylists. Two extra staff were taken on for the world cruises.

The atmosphere in the lower decks was closely knit and even claustrophobic, the Steiner employees being confined to tiny cabins with two or three allocated to each. They would sometimes be forced to sit in a shower stall for some privacy. It was essential to get on with each other, for they were not allowed to mix socially with customers on the upper decks. Life on board did not start well for Susannah, because her East Sheen tones immediately led some female colleagues to decide that she was cool and aloof. Many of them were from northern backgrounds and if they called her 'Suzy', Susannah would correct them by announcing grandly that her name was 'Susannah – with an "H" '. Her accent and manner soon irritated them and they responded by calling her 'H'. The Steiner staff were occasionally required to stage demonstrations upstairs where such accents proliferated, and were free to meet either customers or officers during off-duty hours at ports of call – but much of their lives was spent together in the proletarian crew bars down below.

Here Susannah started to learn an entirely new vocabulary. To be 'shotaway' meant to be drunk or hung over, 'tonks' were homosexuals. Drugs were passed around freely, and a man working in the kitchens was known as 'The Chemist' because of his reputation for producing on demand any known drug. He kept the materials in the ship's refrigerators and because the *QE*2 called at many Third World as well as Western ports, both buying and selling drugs was relatively straightforward. It was a thriving business, but one that did not particularly interest Susannah. She had experimented with cannabis, and a former boyfriend had been an enthusiastic user of 'Whizz', an amphetamine similar to the better-known 'Speed' – but there her involvement in drugs ended.

What did interest Susannah more and more was the opposite sex. She quickly developed a strong sexual drive and lovers found her an eager and willing partner. 'If only they could see me now,' she would say to a boyfriend, referring to her parents and the Putney Set back home in London. A young man to whom she was especially close found Susannah to be sexually 'adventurous'. Her search for a man intensified dramatically on board the *QE*2 and once she left: the days of Baz, the rejected butcher's boy, were long since gone. Before long she had relationships with two waiters. But when it docked in Southampton for a few hours before turning round to other destinations, the faithful Dave Hodgkinson would be there to meet her and they would go to bed-and-breakfast guest houses to be together.

But then Susannah would leave the dreary British winter behind her and sail into hot climates and exotic ports, all the time ministering to rich, mainly American, clients during the days. She would tend to the whims and faces of women like Soraya Khashoggi, estranged wife of the legendary arms dealer, earning an average of £60–70 a week in tips. In the evenings she would frequently dispense drinks at The Hatch, the crowded crew bar that catered for heterosexual men and women. (There was another used predominantly by homosexuals.) In ports she would leave the ship as soon as she was allowed, and once on land she was often mistaken for a passenger. Thankfully discarding her white coat, she sported sunglasses and a Walkman. (Her tastes in music were unremarkable: she liked Joan Armatrading and Lionel Richie.) In wintry New York, she would venture into Manhattan with her Walkman, sunglasses, denim jacket and pink mufflers. For those crew members able to enjoy themselves despite the unglamorous, cramped conditions in which they lived, it was like being on a permanent cruise. Susannah was twenty-two, unusually attractive, and almost literally had the world at her feet. Responsibilities and ties could safely be left behind at home and no one there would find out what had gone on.

She had been aboard the ship for two months, the detectives later learned, when members of the crew held a boisterous Hallowe'en party at The Hatch. Susannah had a lot to drink – she favoured vodka and lime, and at 25p for a double measure of spirits the duty-free drinks on board were extremely cheap – and later had to be helped to bed by the girl with whom she shared a cabin, and by Jon Hall, a twenty-one-year-old Steiner hairdresser and former police cadet. Hall was tall and flamboyant, and Susannah had told friends that she found him attractive and thought that he looked like the lead guitarist of the pop group Duran Duran. Following the noisy party he returned to his cabin, where a group of other men were still up playing cards.

Half an hour later he and others were astonished when Susannah walked in, said nothing, and climbed into bed with Hall. The men playing cards quickly made their excuses and left. Next morning Hall was slightly embarrassed about their passionate nocturnal encounter, but to his surprise she was nonchalant and behaved as though nothing unusual had happened. To him her behaviour seemed a strange reversal of the stereotyped sexual roles, but he was not complaining. That night signalled the start of an intense nine-month relationship with Hall, one that flourished at sea but was doomed to die back in Britain. The two travelled the world together, visiting such exotic locations as the Pyramids in Egypt, and Hawaii, Acapulco, Manila, St Kitts, Mombasa and Bangkok: taking photographs of each other, swimming in clear-blue seas, haggling for fake Rolex and Cartier watches in Hong Kong, getting blissfully shotaway. Back home in East Sheen Avenue the Lamplughs put up a map on their wall, proudly charting the progress of their eldest daughter sailing round the world on the *QE*2 as each hastily scrawled postcard arrived from her.

Before long, Hall had fallen deeply in love with Susannah. He was a year younger than she, his birthday falling on the day after hers. They had a spectacularly successful joint birthday party which lasted until three in the morning at The Hatch, where they soon became a popular and established couple. 'I was as nervous as hell,' Susannah confessed to the *QE*2 diary she kept. Though they each shared cabins with others, they managed to be alone together in one at least every day. The gossip on the ship irritated Susannah, though. She described the *QE*2 as a 'tank of gossip' and complained that 'just because you are friendly to a guy – most of the people on here are men – that means you are "boxed off" – they love to gossip'.

She was very conscious of how the atmosphere on board differed from that of home. Her diary, full of grammatical infelicities and dyslexic misspellings, noted the misgivings she felt: 'We seem to be getting cruder by the minute the language on here I'd never dream to say at home all the boys are so horny & crude so are counting the days to Patia [Pattaya] nookie land also full of diseases.' Their enthusiasm, she later recorded, turned out to have its consequences: 'Roomer has it 400 cases of the dose.' She found 'horny officers' a problem much of the time on board, though her interest in the 'men field' remained: 'Alison and I went out on deck & were suzzing out the tonks from the men which were grately outnumbered.' In another entry she noted: 'We've got some new raving tonks – bloody faggots . . .' A few days later: 'The new tonks seem to be settling in now.'

There were always people in crew quarters smoking (marijuana) or sniffing (cocaine), she complained: 'Not for me, no way.' She found in Mombasa that 'as usual on the dock were millions of stalls and nigers [sic] selling wood carvings . . . could exchange them for . . . Cunard towels'. She and Hall decided they would like to settle in South Africa, perhaps in Cape Town, where they would go into business together. She had been horrified by the sight of people defecating in Indian streets, and thought Egyptians 'slimmy things'.

A year after sailing down the Solent for the first time, Susannah's idyll on the *QE*2 drew to a close. She had clearly enjoyed her experiences travelling around the world. 'I can't believe it,' she wrote at the end of the world cruise. 'One of my ambitions was to travel the world by *QE*2 & I've done it.' She described the day the liner docked in Southampton – 'before we had even landed my family were taking control' – and how excited she was to tell her sisters and parents about her great adventure. There still remained some more routine trips to New York, Florida and Bermuda, but nothing would be the same again after the world cruise in the company of Jon Hall. 'Well I've enjoyed it on here. With the parties, the Hatch, cabin parties, hassles at work, going ashore, windsurfing, being shotaway etc etc.' There was a touching last entry in her seafaring diary: 'I'll definitely miss the crowd on here. They've been like a family to me.'

Back in England Susannah discussed living together with Hall. But she insisted on staying in London, and he wanted to live in the Hertfordshire or Buckinghamshire area. He was unsympathetic to what he called Susannah's 'Hooray Henry' or 'Sloane Ranger' lifestyle, and resumed his old job as a hairdresser at a salon in Beaconsfield. Susannah went to work as a beautician at the Cumberland Hotel near Marble Arch. There, she told Hall, male Arab customers often demanded 'extras' during massages. It did not seem to bother her though he felt certain that she did not supply them. Before long she returned for a couple of weeks to the *QE*2 despite Hall's strong objections. He did not fully trust her, he explained, with such a large and predominantly male crew. She liked the attention of the men on board a little too much, he felt.

It was already clear by now, though, that Susannah was drifting apart from Hall. He, like Baz, did not fit in well at East Sheen Avenue – or with the Putney Set. They did not have a lot of money, he thought, but were living on dreams and pretences. He loathed the prospect of going to events like the Henley Regatta with the upwardly mobile Susannah. She asked him to wear black tie for her friend Sarah 'Puff' Hough's twenty-first birthday at St Katherine's Dock, and he groaned at the screams of delight from the others when a Tarzan kissogram arrived. He felt he had nothing to say to the Putney Set, and drank quietly on his own – much to Susannah's consternation.

He was roped in to one of Diana Lamplugh's Slimnastic presentations too, arriving one morning at 6.30 to help as requested. But he felt that in comparison with the Putney Set, he was not fully welcomed. He normally wore an earring in one ear, but Susannah made him remove it before he saw her parents. Nor did she allow him to smoke in front of them. He was uncomfortable with her family and thought there was little normal affection or openness between mother and daughter; he had never encountered a family like the Lamplughs and found them 'strange'. He did not speak with the same accent as they did. Within weeks Susannah and Hall recognized that they were now leading separate lives, but they made a pact for old times' sake. They would continue to meet each other regularly just for sex, irrespective of who they were going out with at the time.

By now Susannah was twenty-three and again unattached. That Christmas, home on leave from the ship, she went to see Pam Spurr-Seager – the former American client for whom Susannah had performed countless facials and massages. It was an ongoing joke between them that she would call Spurr-Seager 'Pamela Jane' in a fake American Southern twang; Spurr-Seager would always call her 'Susannah Jane' in the same way. But this time she was upset. She had discovered, Susannah told Spurr-Seager at her home, that while she was on the *QE*2 Dave Hodgkinson had been unfaithful to her. He had acquired a new girlfriend: what should she do now? A constant thread in her conversation with Spurr-Seager was the 'tremendous pressure' she felt from her mother to get married – and Spurr-Seager felt it was steadily increasing. 'I envy you, Pam, you've got everything you want,' Susannah told her. The twenty-seven-year-old Californian woman had a wealthy property developer husband, a large and elegant house in a fashionable part of London, and two children, a boy and a girl. To Susannah, it was the perfect combination. A combination of Hodgkinson and Hough – the former's personality, the latter's money – would make the ideal husband for her, she thought. If only Hodge would settle down and get a respectable job . . .

There was absolutely no logical reason why Susannah at this stage in her life *should* have felt she had to look for a husband. She was young, strikingly attractive, ambitious and had unlimited willing escorts. But in the coming months her private life was destined to become increasingly frantic, with much of it staying secret from her family and the Putney Set. She confided in Pam Spurr-Seager about her older boyfriend – whom Spurr-Seager later suspected of being married – and Spurr-Seager was at first delighted. Her own husband was forty-two and was uncomfortable in the company of younger adults like Susannah and her circle. Now, she reasoned, she and her husband would be able to go out in a foursome with Susannah and her new friend. But then Susannah told her that two evenings in succession at the man's luxury flat, he had taken phone calls from a woman. Before long there were no more mentions of the boyfriend from Susannah, and Spurr-Seager did not raise the subject again either.

But the pair continued their close relationship, with Susannah visiting her house as often as four times a week. On Sunday evenings she would give Spurr-Seager a massage, and then they would have a glass of wine together. Sometimes her husband would be there too. Like the wealthy young man who lived in the Bahamas, the Spurr-Seagers provided access to a more affluent, glittering world – just the sort of world of which Susannah so yearned to be part. They took her to the Poppy Ball at the Inter-Continental Hotel in London, when Susannah's partner was an extremely wealthy Arab prince involved in the property market. They got on well together and she left the hotel with him, telling Spurr-Seager afterwards that he had behaved 'like a perfect gentleman'. But she added that her parents would not approve of her going out with an Arab, and again nothing apparently developed.

By this time Susannah was also undecided what to do about work. Beauty therapy was clearly no longer an appropriate occupation for someone with so much social and economic ambition. She asked the owner at Joan Price's Face Place whether she could become a teacher there, but that would have meant a year's course, one night a week, at a polytechnic – and life was too short for that. She applied to British Airways to become a stewardess, but was rejected: perhaps, she thought, because of her dyslexia. Then she landed a job as beautician at the Kensington Hilton, but saw that only as a temporary measure. What she really wanted to do when she returned from the ship was to go into business with Spurr-Seager.

They had discussed many times what sort of enterprise it would be. Susannah would run the beautician side of it, and Spurr-Seager would be concerned with the fitness aspect. The girls would wear glamorous outfits, not the type of pink-and-brown pinafores that had been Susannah's uniform at Joan Price's Face Place. There would be easy, restful decorations. Susannah wanted to call it 'Face Fitness', emphasizing the dual role it would serve, but Spurr-Seager preferred 'Heaven'. The Spurr-Seagers would back the business, but would give Susannah ten per cent of it. And as soon as their daughter Stephanie was no longer an infant, the fantasy could become reality. Pam Spurr-Seager duly started to look at possible sites. At twenty-three Susannah Lamplugh was lessening the gulf between East Sheen Avenue and the likes of Kensington and Chelsea all the time.

Meanwhile her father's mother had died while she was on the *QE*2, leaving money to her grandchildren. The inheritance gave Susannah enough cash to put down a deposit and take out a mortgage on a top-floor two-bedroomed flat in Putney, in Disraeli Road. Her new home gave her a solid base from which to mix with the Putney Set friends whom Hall had found so difficult. Despite their new liaisons she saw Hodgkinson again, and continued sleeping with Hall under their post-*QE*2 pact.

Thoughts and worries about men were never far away. Should she marry, she asked her mother, for love or money? If she was still not married at thirty, she vowed, she would marry Hough.

All this period of Susannah Lamplugh's life greatly interested the detectives. With the help of Cunard's security department in Southampton, they began the long and laborious process of checking Susannah's male colleagues on the *QE*2 – cross-referencing to see if those who had been with her on the ship at any time also happened to be on leave in England the day she disappeared. It was a long shot, but worth trying. Even if the system threw up a name, however, the likelihood of being able to produce any incriminating evidence was fading fast. The police team was still trying hard, working such long hours that Detective Superintendent Carter had to insist that they took days off. Families were beginning to become involved too. 'Daddy has still not found Mrs Lamploo,' wrote Detective Inspector Johnstone's seven-year-old daughter in her school news book.

Because of Susannah's flourishing private life, the task of tracking down possible witnesses and then taking signed statements – even from men who had been intimate with her – became a major undertaking for the police. The detectives were also finding it difficult to talk to the Putney Set: on a human level they had little in common, and did not share the same interests in property prices, windsurfing and partying. There was no question but that the young men and women wanted to help, but the police found them peculiarly unforthcoming. No one seemed able to give them any really helpful information about Susannah's habits and movements. The friends all appeared very similar, and one policeman wearily described them as 'clones'. 'If they keep saying the same things about her, I'll go MAD,' another frustrated, irate detective screamed at colleagues across the incident room after a long day.

Finally, Detective Superintendent Carter decided to play a critical new card. Forty detectives working furiously hard had been unable to solve the case over several weeks, so why not ask 55 million to play detective too? He made a crucial decision that he had been considering for some time: he would appeal to the mass public for help through the BBC television programme *Crimewatch UK*. It could rebound on the police, because there would inevitably be a flood of information and every accusation and detail would then have to be checked. That all took enormous time and resources, but it took only one correct clue to lead to the man ... If 'Mr Kipper' existed, someone somewhere must know all about him and might even be shielding him. Had he perhaps met Susannah sometime between the end of her time on the *QE*2 and the day she disappeared? For the police were beginning to show more and more interest in that crucial period.

Chapter Eight

Before long Diana Lamplugh found that persistent urge returning. She just had to *do* something. Sitting at home talking to the media was not enough, and all the publicity in the world had still not found her daughter. For some time she had been able only to look on while the police told her of their concern about a luxury block of flats in Stevenage Road, close to where Susannah's office car had been found. Was it possible that whoever had abandoned the car in Stevenage Road had then gone to a flat in the same road with Susannah? That such a person might even live in one of the flats? In the popular imagination, the police could burst in anywhere and then interrogate a suspect until he confessed. But in the real world, they could search private property without the owner's consent only with warrants – and to get those warrants, they needed evidence.

So Diana Lamplugh decided to take matters into her own hands. She was the only person who would be able to by-pass these procedures, she decided. She would search the flats *herself*. She formed a plan without telling the police: she and a friend would go to the flats in the guise of journalists, she as a writer and he as a photographer. They would disguise themselves with dark glasses and hats, taking enough money to bribe the flats' caretaker. And, in case there was any trouble, they would also take a gun. She had found the gun during the great garage clear-out, but made one mistake in her planning. She discussed taking the gun during conversations on the phone, forgetting that the police were still taping every call. It embarrassed her, but the police were to take no action.

In the event, the money was not necessary either. The caretaker was willingly co-operative and immediately agreed to Diana Lamplugh's unusual request – to drain the building's sumps to establish that her daughter's body was not dumped there. They all then peered expectantly into the murky tanks, and were relieved to find no bodies. They climbed countless stairs too, looking into flats and at one point disturbing someone whom Diana Lamplugh thought was a prostitute in the midst of plying her trade. She decided several people at the flats needed further attention: one an African chieftain who apparently had a police record and had been in prison, a valet called Pedro, a Chinese chauffeur, and an Arab who had supposedly at some point done business with Sturgis. She gave the police all the details but they came up against their predictable problem: there was no evidence to link any of these men with Susannah Lamplugh or her disappearance. The clandestine operation came to nothing, and wearily Diana Lamplugh and the friend made their way back to East Sheen Avenue with the mystery still unsolved.

Friends kept telling the Lamplughs that they must not give up hope. They always agreed, as though to give up hope would somehow be disloyal to Susannah. But inwardly each knew there was little or no chance their daughter was alive, and that the other felt the same way. Sometimes they would cling to each other wordlessly in their grief. One morning Paul Lamplugh got up as usual to make his wife breakfast and found himself in floods of tears for virtually the first time since he became an adult. 'Why has it happened? I don't understand,' he kept repeating, pacing up and down the kitchen and feeling utterly distraught. In private Diana Lamplugh too would burst into tears, in marked contrast to her controlled public appearances. '*It's so awful*,' she would say to her husband. No words seemed adequate.

The way she had frequently expressed herself was by writing those long and sometimes fraught family newsletters, articulating emotions that were less apparent when she spoke. Her son urged her to continue writing the letters, putting the awful events down on paper. Three weeks after her daughter disappeared she duly sat down at her desk and tapped out on her portable typewriter four words: 'My dearest darling Suzy'. There then followed more than thirteen sides of a single-spaced typewritten letter to Susannah, telling her of the events following her disappearance in the inimitable style that had become so familiar to the family. It was completed over the next fortnight. Their lives had been completely changed (probably for good) and they all missed her so much, Mrs Lamplugh wrote: 'We partly miss you because you would be so enjoying it all! In so short a time you have achieved the kind of fame people work towards for a lifetime and also engendered the love and admiration of so many people you have never even met or heard of and will probably never know.'

She told of how she had been to Susannah's flat in Disraeli Road: 'I went with Katie and Puff to clear up your flat and I found it so very very hard. I was so pleased that they were with me. It [is] such a super flat and everything you have done in it has been so successful. I looked at your pictures, your photos, your macreme [*sic*], your dresses you have and are making, your birthday cards . . . it all looked so happy, so successful, so innocent, so wrong, so wrong that you were no longer there.' She described in characteristic whirlwind detail the dealings with the police, media, television organizations, and with Mary Asprey and her mediums. She wrote too of the trivial, the family domestic life which she could no longer share with Susannah: 'Our room is going to be heaven, melon walls, curtains cream lace on melon lining . . . daddy's study will have the same green carpet as Lizzie and so I have got sage green on cream wallpaper (very pretty and masculine) . . . it should all look marvellous.'

She wanted to bring her daughter up to date with other family news she had missed: 'By the time Daddy came to take his interview he was in a high old state.' When Mrs Lamplugh finally completed the letter she handed it to her husband, as usual, to duplicate and circulate. Then she gave it to *The Standard* in London, which reprinted parts of it. The *Daily Telegraph, Mirror* and *Star* followed suit, and after describing it as 'a poignant, moving letter' BBC television news showed film of Mrs Lamplugh apparently typing it at her desk. Caroline Davies, *The Standard*'s reporter who more than any other journalist had made the Lamplugh story her own, was subsequently offered a staff job by the paper.

But for the Lamplughs there was no end to the agony. Instead of getting better, the lack of firm news meant the wait was becoming worse. The most emotional ordeal that faced them was returning to Ondara, the family holiday home near Newport in Wales. Here the Lamplughs shared their fondest memories of their daughter from early in her life: windsurfing in her wet suit, sailing, organizing family events, pepping up the others. Had she not disappeared, Susannah would have joined the rest of the family at the house for the August bank holiday weekend. Should they all still go to Wales, deserting the telephone and the family home that was waiting for Susannah in case she returned? Paul and Diana Lamplugh were the most reluctant, but their children and friends of Susannah like Adam Leegood,

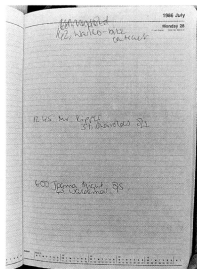

The fateful appointment in Susannah Lamplugh's diary (*above*), and the estate agent's office in Fulham Road (*below*) which she left apparently to meet 'Mr Kipper'.

Susannah Lamplugh's Ford Fiesta double-parked outside 37 Shorrolds Road during a police reconstruction of her possible movements (*above*). Her car was found abandoned more than a mile away in Stevenage Road, partially blocking a garage entrance. Her straw hat was still on the back ledge.

Police and dog-handlers search open ground (*above*), and an incident room (*below*) was set up almost immediately.

Paul and Diana Lamplugh and Adam Leegood answer questions outside Fulham police station the day after Susannah disappeared (*above*), and Detective Superintendent Nick Carter (*far left*) and Detective Inspector Peter Johnstone confer at the Lamplugh Squad headquarters. Detective Inspector Johnstone regularly kept Diana Lamplugh in touch with the police operation (*above right*) and police issued two impressions of 'Mr Kipper' (*right*). *Far right*: the last known picture of Susannah Lamplugh, taken at a party two nights before she disappeared.

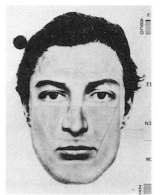

Diana Lamplugh consoles her daughter Tamsin, the elder of Susannah's two sisters and her closest confidante, shortly after she arrived from New Zealand.

Living life to the full: Susannah Lamplugh enjoyed outdoor sports, especially swimming and windsurfing.

Three hundred came to the retirement party for Detective Superintendent Nick Carter (*above*, *kneeling second from right*), including Diana, Paul and Tamsin Lamplugh and Mary Asprey (*far right*). The Lamplugh inquiry was the only murder investigation he left unsolved. *Below*: the Lamplughs at peace: from left, Tamsin, Elizabeth, Richard, Diana and Paul Lamplugh. On the floor, Leo, the retriever, and Snoopy, the cocker spaniel.

Dave Hodgkinson and the Houghs persuaded them that they should go.

Their van broke down on the way, and they arrived late in the evening. Next morning it was a warm day and the tide was high; the family and their usual entourage of young adults had their breakfast on the wall looking out to sea and remembering Susannah. Passers-by stopped to shake their hands and told them: 'We are so glad you came. Thank you for coming.' There was no wind for surfing, and Tamsin and Dave Hodgkinson went swimming instead. Others got out boats and canoes, and Paul and Diana Lamplugh drove off alone to buy some newspapers. A typical Ondara weekend was under way – but with one member of the party conspicuously absent. Hodgkinson especially found it all very difficult.

Then the phone rang. It was the *Mail on Sunday*, wanting to take a photograph of the group. The Lamplughs and their missing daughter were still major news in Britain, and for a national newspaper a photograph of the group on holiday meant something of a scoop. With a Fleet Street style redolent of days gone by, the paper sent their men not by car or train but by *helicopter*. To everyone's disbelief it started chugging distantly over the mountains, gradually coming closer until it finally landed in a patch of gorse not far from the house. Two photographers emerged, climbed over a five-bar gate, marshalled the group and took the picture that was later to appear prominently in the newspaper. Then they left and the helicopter again became a distant speck in the sky. It was yet another surreal incident, ordinary lives touched by the melodramatic urgency of the media.

That weekend Tamsin Lamplugh was especially conscious of the effect Susannah's disappearance was having on her parents, and the role she could play to help them. She knew that her father had enjoyed sailing with Susannah and so offered to go out in a boat with him instead. It was while he was sailing with Tamsin as his unaccustomed crewmate that the tragedy of what had happened suddenly struck Lamplugh once again, this time with horrible force. This wasn't Suzy facing him across the boat as usual: it was Tamsin, and Suzy was never coming back. She had probably gone for ever. Father and second daughter returned sadly to the shore, and Paul Lamplugh went upstairs. There, alone, he broke down.

In the kitchen Diana Lamplugh heard what she described as a 'yelp', and rushed up to be with her husband. She decided to bring Tamsin and Richard up too – she felt her youngest daughter Elizabeth could not take such grief – and there Lamplugh shared his torment with them. It turned out to be a helpful experience for him, and he said afterwards that he felt 'cleansed'. That evening he made a speech at the communal Ondara supper, toasting Susannah once again and telling her friends that they could always come to Wales and be part of the extended family. By confronting the realization that Susannah would not be there, Diana Lamplugh said later in a postscript to her letter, they had made it easier to return to Wales.

Throughout this time the police, she told Susannah in the letter, had been 'marvellous'. She described her visit to the incident room which she found 'incredibly impressive':

There was an Office Manager, two girl WPCs answering the phone (which rang consistently), two girl WPCs sorted the calls into Priority, down to low Priority, then on to a Detective who decided which to action, on to the Detectives (35 of them) to carry this through, on to the 6 Detectives who indexed the information and cross-referenced it, on to the Manager again who read through the reports as they came in, back to the Action-Detective who decided if more was needed and back to the

Referencing section and up to the DI in charge and if necessary on to the Big White Chief (who rings us every night and when needs be) and sometimes to the BIGGER White Chief who runs their Think Tank each evening. Occasionally they are visited by the even BIGGER Chieftain who has Sir David Napley and us on his tail. They have done everything – dredged the Thames, sent down the frogmen, combed the Parks with dogs and horses, searched all the gardens and houses in the Area and all the empty houses for Sale just outside it; they have interviewed all your workmates, and all your friends and EVERYONE in your diary, and all your acquaintances and even those who have only seen or met you once. They have searched the QEII, they have sent Interpol to see [X] in Barbados, they have given [Y] a difficult time, they have been super to us. They have done so much, they have tried so hard, but they have found absolutely nothing. I cannot understand, we cannot understand, they cannot understand why we cannot find you – where are you darling? We look at everyone going around London and wonder why, why you? It all makes no sense at all.

But the detectives were still being discreet about what they told the Lamplughs, for virtually every day they were discovering things about Susannah's life that they felt were better left unsaid to her parents. Because of the remarkably successful way she seemed to have handled her money, they had even been considering whether Susannah might have been involved in prostitution before her disappearance. If she had been, that would clearly put a very different light on the case. A former boyfriend was asked outright by detectives if he thought Susannah had been what they called 'tomming it', and another suggested to them unequivocally that he suspected she had. But there was no evidence whatsoever to support the idea. The investigating team carefully examined Susannah's bank account statements, and found no money had been paid in which they could not explain. From then on, the theory was dropped.

What still interested the detectives greatly were the two years of Susannah's life ending shortly before her disappearance. It was now likely, they felt, that if a kidnapper had abducted her he would be someone she had met during this period. But where? They soon established that after working at the Cumberland Hotel, Susannah had obtained a job as a beautician at the Kensington Hilton. She worked there for several months until she was almost twenty-four, but was not content either with the lifestyle or money. She was ambitious: she told a friend that she would have a Mercedes in three years, and knew exactly which model too. Then, one winter's day early in 1985, she found what she was looking for. She walked into the Fulham office of Sturgis and Son, a firm of estate agents with branches mainly in south and west London and a staff of more than a hundred. 'My name's Susannah Lamplugh,' she told the manager, Mark Gurdon. 'I want a job as a negotiator.' Gurdon was so impressed that he offered her a job almost immediately.

For someone with Susannah's ambitions, the new job was ideal. She would be selling property in a fast-moving jungle of flats and houses in west London, and with her basic salary and commission she could hope to make at least £12,000 a year – considerably more than her previous earnings as a beautician. Her youngest sister Elizabeth, then fifteen, had earlier started the tradition of sending out personalized Christmas cards that humorously depicted the past year of each member of the family. That year the Lamplugh family Christmas card showed the eldest daughter with one arm around a Sturgis 'Sold' sign, and what the card said was an extract from *The Official Sloane Ranger Handbook*: 'If you have the gift of the gab and a shade more ambition than most SRs, an estate agent opens exactly the right door: you can become a negotiator . . . salespersons

Sloanes, all telephoning and seeing clients noisily at once . . .'
The extract was captioned 'Susannah at Work?'

Joining Sturgis was the second turning point in Susannah Lamplugh's life. She became much more self-assured: colleagues found that she was an exceptionally able negotiator who soon learned the tricks of the estate agent's trade. She started talking about the fast cars she would buy. She often took only part of her lunch break lest she miss a call that could lead to a commission. In the summer she played tennis with colleagues, and frequently joined them at the Crocodile Tears wine bar across the road from the office. She became a familiar young-woman-about-town, every day driving her new white company car around the area to show houses and flats to clients. To all appearances she was in the prime of her life, and men found her highly attractive. A young uniformed policeman who spotted her driving her car in Fulham once pulled her over for some imaginary offence, precisely for an opportunity to speak to her.

For her twenty-fourth birthday her parents took her to Harrods for pink champagne and smoked salmon sandwiches. She was living life at a fast pace, working hard, socializing with clients, eating and drinking with the Putney Set, regularly meeting new boyfriends, visiting nightclubs – and still finding the time to see her family. In the evenings she would eat at fashionable west London establishments like Little Italy, Tootsies, or Pizza Mia. Later she might go on to Tokyo Joe, a Piccadilly discothèque. Within the Putney Set a tradition developed whereby members would use an exercise book to sign-in, and make additional comments during their evenings of social drinking. Though many of the remarks besides the names were juvenile and vulgar, Susannah's entry would be businesslike: 'Suz Lamplugh' under 'Name' and 'Woman' under 'Rank' (changed on that particular page to 'Wank').

Her weekends and holidays were equally hectic. She spent one weekend playing war games with a male friend, in which opposing teams of twenty pretended to fire real bullets and tried to capture the other's flags – but she found it expensive and vowed not to return. She went skiing in France for a week when a dozen members of the Set rented a villa. She spent a weekend in Paris with Leegood. In London she continued to have relationships with Hall, Hodgkinson and Hough. She went to a 'shirts and sunglasses' party attended by other estate agents not long before she disappeared. It was all go, but she rarely seemed tired. (The night before she disappeared was an exception: she told her parents then that she was 'knackered'.)

Throughout this period she was a popular, successful young woman whom hardly anyone disliked. Friends found that she had that rare and enviable human quality: she made them feel better when she was around them. Her presence at parties was such that people would want to know who she was, what her name was, what she did for a living. 'Bubbly' was a word often used to describe her personality. She seemed always to have *time* for friends and family, specially visiting her grandmother to spend time with her even in the midst of a hectic lifestyle. She never seemed to have a bad word to say about anyone, and always took an interest in what others were doing. She would happily give up a day off to drive a friend round London to help him look for a flat. To her friends and family, Susannah Lamplugh was special.

But there was also a less happy side to her. She seemed to be on a permanent, lonely quest for sexual fulfilment. No one man seemed to satisfy her and she could not form any lasting relationship. Men told her that they were in love with her, but she seemed unable to reciprocate.

Numerous lovers drifted in and out of her life during this time. They were invariably professional men in their twenties or thirties, tall and conventionally handsome. The encounters were nevertheless doomed to fail. They could be impulsive: young men later told the police how she would sleep with them after their first evening together. The gossip among fellow estate agents was that she was proud that she had not been rejected by any of her many lovers. She, it was said, was the one who did the rejecting. But she managed to stay on good terms with former boyfriends none the less.

It did not take the police long to realize that such an involved personal life could have a bearing on her disappearance. They had begun to be aware of it the day after Susannah's disappearance, and it soon became an important factor in the investigation. Even if she had not met her abductor beforehand, they theorized, she *might* have readily agreed to go off to lunch, say, with 'Mr Kipper'. The reverse could also have been true, but the detectives had to consider all the possibilities. Tracing all Susannah's secret contacts, sexual and otherwise, was complex work, and before long the investigating team decided that there had been so many men in her life that they would take statements from only a selection of them. There was no reason to suspect any of the men who had been unearthed in the inquiry so far, though they were keen to know more about the wealthy young man who lived alternately in Park Lane and the Bahamas. Later he too was cleared.

The Lamplugh family knew that Susannah was sexually active. Years before, when she was a teenager, her mother had discussed with her the methods of contraception she should use. But they had no idea of the extent of her sex life, and the detectives had to tread carefully when talking to the parents: they were going through enough trauma as it was, without being unnecessarily upset. Much later, Paul and Diana Lamplugh were shocked when they found out what people were saying about their daughter. The young woman leading a secret and sometimes lonely life was not the young woman they knew and loved.

Their ordeal, it was becoming clear, was all the more harrowing because it had no end in sight. Normal bereavements fell into a pattern of initial shock, mourning and gradual recovery – but in this case all such reactions were inevitably blurred and unresolved. They could not mourn because there was hope that Susannah might still be alive, that she might not have been abducted – and if they did not hold on to that hope, they felt guilty. It was a time of torment for all the family.

But as the memorably warm summer drew to a close, they had no choice but to try to rebuild their lives. Paul Lamplugh's interview at the Law Society – the one for which Susannah had wished him luck at their last meeting – turned out to be successful, and he started heading a new department thirty-four days after his daughter disappeared. He and his wife went to Sicily for a week's holiday. Tamsin Lamplugh gave her first dinner party and resumed work with the international hotel agency, this time in their London office. (Before long the organization, like so many others, would be taken over by Rupert Murdoch.) Elizabeth, now sixteen, returned from her Far East trip optimistically bringing a gift of pearls for Susannah. Then she had her hair permed at Harrods and prepared to start the autumn term as one of twenty-two girls among a hundred and ten boys at Cheltenham College.

For Diana Lamplugh the position was different, for there was less routine in her life and no full-time job to propel her along. She resumed her Slimnastics and swimming classes, working 19 hours a week, and that helped. But now her daughter's disappearance had made her a public personality as well, and a new way of life was developing for her. Her youngest daughter had chosen not to appear on television to talk about her sister, despite requests. Tamsin had done so, but her appearances had fitted the more usual pattern of a reluctant and tongue-tied relative discussing a subject that deeply moved her. Paul Lamplugh had tended to appear on television only as a support to his wife, who did nearly all the talking. But Diana Lamplugh, always snappily dressed, was now a regular sight on British television screens. She was a natural television performer: often live in the studio, always appearing confident and with a familiar half-smile on her face, talking in an apparently cool and unemotional way about her missing daughter. Back in East Sheen Avenue, the Lamplughs kept videos of the television appearances.

There had never been a case quite like the Lamplugh one before, and the public was fascinated by it – both by the mystery of what had happened to Susannah, and by Diana Lamplugh's striking personality. The publicity meant that countless people contacted the Lamplughs to discuss the case: friends, neighbours, self-professed mediums and the disturbed, other victims' families, and famous as well as ordinary people. Relatives seemed to find it most difficult of all. One of Diana Lamplugh's brothers, who lived with his family in Germany, said he would come to East Sheen Avenue 'when necessary'. She felt it was necessary there and then, but did not tell him so.

The calls continued. A typical example came one day from the Reverend Dr Colin Morris, former President of the Methodist Conference and a distinguished religious broadcaster who had taken an interest in the case. 'Can I come and see you?' he asked Mrs Lamplugh. The case had caught his imagination, he explained when he met her, and he felt he just had to talk to her. Then Diana Lamplugh told him how much she was *enjoying* the media appearances, and how guilty that made her feel. 'I hate to say this,' replied Morris, 'but I think you've been trained for this moment. *Get on and do it.*' Ever since her daughter had disappeared, Diana Lamplugh's instinct was that she had to keep all the publicity going in the effort to find her. If she failed to do so, she felt, Susannah's life would simply go out like a flame. It would be a *waste*. She reminded herself that Dr Desmond Kelly, the Harley Street psychiatrist who went to the same church, had advised her to throw herself into some kind of work.

Before the end of the first month, she had begun to devise a plan. 'I think', she wrote in her now famous letter to her daughter, 'you have started something which is now rolling and will not stop – it's fascinating that something good might grow out of such a terrible sacrifice – the TV programme went well at TV AM (at least Granny enjoyed it), tomorrow I have a radio interview with BBC Wales and a Feature for the Express . . .' What Diana Lamplugh decided to do in the midst of so much activity was to find a way of keeping the memory of her daughter alive: The Suzy Lamplugh Trust was the outcome. It would continue 'even if you come swanning back from the Caribeann [*sic*]'. She hoped it would be able to institute research to create some guidelines 'for the working woman and her boss'. The rest of the money, if enough could be raised, would go to 'helping anyone who is going through our kind of traumas (heaven help them) by giving them some kind of support – it has helped so much to keep us sane and alive'.

In the coming months the formation of The Suzy Lamplugh

Trust and its launch would fully occupy Diana Lamplugh. Perhaps, she thought, the Duchess of York – the former Sarah Ferguson, who had been popularly known as Fergie even before her marriage to the Duke of York five days prior to Susannah's disappearance – would agree to become President. That would give the organization royal patronage. But although Buckingham Palace did not accept the invitation Diana Lamplugh went on to compile a long list of trustees, consultants and no fewer than fifty patrons. Baroness Ewart-Biggs, the widow of a British ambassador who was killed by a landmine as he left his Dublin residence a decade before, became a trustee. A woman police inspector (not involved in the Lamplugh case) agreed to become a consultant. Actors, television personalities and politicians joined the list of patrons. Major-General Sir Jeremy Moore (who had commanded the British forces in the Falklands War), Dr Desmond Kelly, Viscountess Astor, Dr Colin Morris, Rabbi Julia Neuberger, Rear-Admiral Martin La Touche Wemyss, Esther Rantzen, Claire Rayner, Desmond Wilcox . . . the list went on and on. There was hardly anyone in the world, it seemed, who was not fascinated by, and concerned about, the Suzy Lamplugh case.

For the Lamplughs the formation of the Trust helped to make sense out of the disappearance of their daughter. She would, in one way or another, live on. 'Life goes on and on,' Diana Lamplugh ended the letter Susannah would almost certainly never see: '. . . It promises to be full and interesting, progressive and necessary . . . I do hope, so hope you come back and enjoy it . . . but one thing darling I am sure your life will prove to have been more than worth while and no one will ever forget you, you'll be part of so many hearts for ever . . .'

But not all Susannah's friends were convinced the formation of the Trust was a good idea. Sarah 'Puff' Hough, perhaps her closest girlfriend after Tamsin, tried to persuade Diana Lamplugh not to proceed with the plan. Susannah, she said, would *hate* the idea of such a public organization established in her name. The two surviving Lamplugh sisters were not clear what the purpose of the Trust was either. Other relatives had mixed feelings about the Trust and Mrs Lamplugh's role in it. Even Diana Lamplugh herself later confessed that her daughter would probably be opposed to it all. But she was determined to set up the Trust, she explained, for Suzy. Out of something terrible would come good, and her life would not be a waste.

None of the senior police team involved in the case joined the Trust either as trustees, consultants, or patrons – and that included Detective Superintendent Carter, who was about to retire and would shortly have time on his hands. They were working as hard as ever at their Kensington headquarters, but were becoming conscious that soon colleagues would probably start to suggest that the inquiry be run down. Twenty-five thousand people went missing in Britain every year, but the extraordinary media attention given to the Lamplugh case meant that the police had been able to devote far more time and resources to it than they would have dreamed. Even the most similar case in recent years – that of Martin Allen, a fifteen-year-old boy who disappeared in London on Guy Fawkes day in 1979 and was never seen again – had attracted nothing like the attention. Carter had worked on that case too, and knew the frustrations involved.

But there was massive public goodwill in the Lamplugh case. Everybody, policeman and civilian, wanted to solve the mystery – and in the existing climate any senior Metropolitan Police officer who ordered the case to be closed would be either a courageous or foolhardy man. And so, many weeks afterwards, the inquiry continued to grow with a momentum all its own. Detectives took careful statements from members of the Putney Set who had been skiing with Susannah in Val-d'Isère the previous winter. With several past and present lovers in the male contingent, had something happened there? They asked Interpol to grill the wealthy young man in the Bahamas about *his* movements on crucial days. They established that Susannah had been mixing with a group of people from the *QE*2 only a month before her disappearance, when she and Hall spent the weekend in Leeds to attend the wedding of friends from the ship.

That alone opened entirely new possibilities. Had Susannah perhaps resumed a relationship with someone she had known on the *QE*2 more than two years before? The patient cross-referencing, with the help of Cunard's security division, continued. The Lamplugh squad were as determined as ever to get their man, and thought there was every possibility that they still would. In East Sheen Avenue Diana Lamplugh busied herself with plans for The Suzy Lamplugh Trust, and mother and daughter were now more famous than ever.

But any clues as to what had happened to Susannah Lamplugh, the attractive twenty-five-year-old who the media said had no problems and no grey areas in her life, were as elusive as ever. Nearly three months after she disappeared, millions of television viewers sat down to watch *Crimewatch*. They saw a reconstruction of Susannah's movements on the day she disappeared, followed by a heartfelt appeal for the public to come forward with information. Had anyone seen this young woman with a man who looked like 'Mr Kipper'? Had they been in Shorrolds Road or Stevenage Road and seen anything suspicious? In the film Woman Detective Constable Barbara Harrison played the role of one of the housewives who had spotted Susannah's car in Stevenage Road. While it was being transmitted throughout the country Detective Superintendent Carter, Detective Inspector Johnstone and Detective Sergeant Barley sat with other police colleagues in the television studio waiting for the calls from potential new witnesses. The moment the programme ended, the phones started to ring furiously.

Chapter Nine

Susannah Lamplugh left no will. Neither did she contribute to any pension funds or have any life insurance. Her flat in Disraeli Road was mortgaged to a building society, and each succeeding month a further repayment was due – but Susannah was no longer present to pay the money. She had put the flat on the market, but it was still unsold at the time of her disappearance. In the eyes of the law at least, Susannah was still alive.

Within three months Paul and Diana Lamplugh had to face another agonizing dilemma. Should they allow their daughter's flat to be sold? Technically, the building society would first repossess it, as it held the deeds to the flat. If neither Susannah nor her body was found, the profits from the sale of the flat together with any other money belonging to Susannah would under law be kept in a trust fund for seven years. Then she could be declared as having died intestate, and her estate could be distributed among her family as next of kin. The Lamplughs decided in the end to proceed with the sale of the flat. They were comforted by the knowledge that Susannah herself was planning to sell it and had agreed an asking price of £73,950. It was what Suzy wanted, they felt.

But Tamsin Lamplugh found it all more difficult. She resented seeing her sister's jewellery distributed among the mediums and clairvoyants in the hope that from it they could get a 'feel' for Susannah. She did not think it right that her mother or anyone else should go through Susannah's belongings. She knew it was inevitable and perhaps even reasonable that they should, but felt a deep instinct for protecting her sister and her belongings from others. They were Susannah's things, and not to be fingered by some self-professed medium or clairvoyant she had never even met.

In the event, it was Paul Lamplugh who found it most difficult to go to Susannah's flat. Her mother and Tamsin finally went themselves, and as unemotionally as they could proceeded to dismantle the daily realities of Susannah's life. Clothes, jewellery, ornaments, beds, plants, all were packed away and many of the belongings then stored in the Lamplughs' loft in East Sheen Avenue. It was as poignant an acknowledgement as could be that the family did not expect Susannah back – although for many months to come, Tamsin would continue to refer to her sister in the present tense. But gradually, over the following year, Susannah's belongings would be distributed. Clothes would go to Tamsin and cousins, pictures to Adam Leegood, and some furniture to Tamsin and an aunt. Two beds went to Tamsin's new flat, and some of the rest of the furniture was sold with the flat. Dave Hodgkinson asked especially if he could have Susannah's plants. To him they were a living, growing reminder of the woman he loved and the times they spent together.

But before the flat was sold, the Lamplughs' tireless helper Mary Asprey organized a group of mediums to gather there and see if they could somehow deduce Susannah's whereabouts from the atmosphere. The police were sceptical, to say the least, about the usefulness of the mediums. Detective Superintendent Carter had never known of any police investigation which had been helped by such people. But the Lamplughs and Mary Asprey hoped that such a disparate group, each claiming special powers, might be able to provide vital clues. There was a tense atmosphere in Susannah's flat when all the mediums finally met, and before long they started arguing with each other. Each claimed to have the most authoritative version of what had happened to Susannah. 'She was buying a house for someone else,' one would say. 'She never drove the car from Sturgis in the first place,' insisted another.

Like most of the other theories coming from the mediums, such notions were perfectly plausible. One of the mediums told Mary Asprey that Susannah had never found a man who could satisfy her - until three months before her disappearance. There were so many theories that the police told themselves that when the mystery was solved, there would be at least *one* medium who would coincidentally have managed to outline all the right details. But inevitably the last meeting in Susannah Lamplugh's flat did not lead to any breakthroughs in the case. The Lamplughs arranged for all Susannah's mail to be redirected to East Sheen Avenue. There was a sense of finality about it all.

By now the Lamplugh family had discovered that there were six identifiable stages to their ordeal. First came what Diana Lamplugh called *total horror*, when they felt 'overheated' and furiously energetic. That reaction was followed closely and unexpectedly by *guilt*. They had the feeling that they should be miserable all the time and permanently solemn about what had happened to Susannah. But sometimes that did not happen, and they just wanted to laugh and joke. With that came a haunting guilt.

Then there was *release*, when they realized it was all right occasionally to be lighthearted – even about Susannah herself. Three or four weeks later came more *worry*, and with it the overriding fear that Susannah was being held somewhere, was in great danger, and needed the urgent help of her parents to escape. They felt they should not be sitting at home, but walking or driving around looking constantly for their daughter. That feeling then gave way to *hope*, that no news was good news and that Susannah must therefore be alive and well. Finally came *acceptance* – that their daughter was probably dead, although simultaneously they wanted to avoid any confirmation of that news. In a way they both wanted it and dreaded it.

The worst moment in the early months came when Detective Inspector Johnstone phoned them to say that the skinned torso of a young woman had been discovered in Sussex. He thought it unlikely that the remains were those of Susannah, but wanted to warn them because the media would inevitably make a link with the Lamplugh case and then ask them their reaction. The partial corpse was meanwhile being subjected to stringent forensic testing and was being genetically 'fingerprinted' for evidence.

From the tests detectives in Sussex soon established two definite facts about the mysterious body. They not only knew the woman's blood group but were also able to tell that she had had either a baby or an abortion. They also learned from the femur bone of the girl that she had probably been 5 feet 2 inches tall – appreciably shorter than Susannah. Diana Lamplugh felt confident that Susannah could never have had a baby or an abortion without her knowing, so that thought partly relieved the Lamplughs too. But she tortured herself by believing that the police would want to dress the corpse in Susannah's clothes to see if they fitted. This course of action had never even been considered by police, but the image had taken root in Mrs Lamplugh's mind. She also told a television interviewer that she would be willing to go through with identifying the remains, though for obvious reasons this too was never a realistic option.

The police team had never been able to establish Susannah's blood group, despite detailed inquiries with doctors and at hospitals and clinics where she had received medical treatment. In order to try to rule out any connection with the torso, Paul and Diana Lamplugh were each asked to give a sample of their blood – so that at least it could possibly be established that the torso was *not* their daughter. It was a memorable low for them at the time. Both went to their local police station where a police surgeon extracted blood from them in a typically unprepossessing police interview room. It took a month from first knowing of the existence of the torso before they were satisfied it was definitely not that of their daughter. Later it was established that the victim was a young Asian woman who had been murdered by members of her own family.

Other lows would hit the family unexpectedly. The wedding of friends in Bedfordshire reduced Diana Lamplugh to tears later in the evening. The bridegroom had known Susannah when both were children, and at the age of twelve they had declared undying love for each other though they had not been close when they were older. Diana Lamplugh had so wanted her daughter to be married, but the reality of this happy family wedding brought home to her that she would never be able to attend the wedding of her eldest daughter. The realization hurt bitterly, and she wept that night.

Back at the Kensington incident room, the police team busily sifted through the information flooding in following the *Crimewatch* programme. The phones were ringing continually. 'Hallo, Lamplugh inquiry,' echoed through the building. The television programme had given an impetus to the inquiry just when it seemed to be flagging. Then, suddenly, one of the calls had everyone in the room taking notice. It seemed to be the breakthrough Carter and his team had hoped for – just one priceless phone call out of the countless well-meaning but ultimately unhelpful calls, the one that would solve the mystery.

The woman at the other end said she was a thirty-three-year-old bookshop manageress calling from near Leeds. She spoke quietly and assuredly, and seemed quite genuine. But she sounded extremely worried and upset.

She had seen the *Crimewatch* programme, she told the young detective who answered the call, and had immediately made a horrific deduction. Suddenly she had realized that she was sheltering the likely abductor and murderer of Susannah Lamplugh. She failed to make the necessary deductions at the time, but having seen the programme it was now all overwhelmingly clear. She explained that she had a young woman lodger, and the lodger had a boyfriend who was an unemployed chef from Middlesbrough. She could be certain of the day: on Monday 28 July the boyfriend had been to London for the day, and came back to the house in the evening with bloodstains on his clothing and a partly consumed bottle of champagne. At the time she had thought they could have been chocolate stains, but now realized they were blood. He went straight to the bathroom to change and wash. *And* he was clutching a bright yellow key fob, and some Sturgis house literature, she now recalled. She was heartbroken but sure he was their man.

Such calls were not unusual for the police, but this one was clearly different. The woman sounded balanced, and from what she said seemed to have no ulterior motive for accusing the man. Immediately Detective Sergeant Barley and a detective constable were dispatched on a train to Leeds, where they went straight to see the woman. She was as they expected, and bore no obvious signs of being under any delusions. She began to cry as they interviewed her. Then they turned their attentions to the chef, who in just a matter of hours had become one of the best suspects they had ever had. He turned out to be twenty-two, of slight build, a fresh-faced teetotaller – and certainly no 'Mr Kipper' lookalike.

Very quickly it became clear to them that the man was also totally innocent. They checked his diary, and spoke at length to his girlfriend – and everything suggested that the man had *not* been in London that day. Barley's policeman instincts also told him the man was innocent, and next day he and his disappointed colleague returned to London. Quite why the bookshop manageress had been so certain was never explained, but they accepted that she was acting in good faith. She had simply done what a surprising number of otherwise balanced and normal people do: they think about a case so much that they convince themselves they have vital information. For Barley and his colleague it had been just another forty-eight hours in the life of the Lamplugh squad.

The detectives persisted with their work, even though each separate line of inquiry could take many hours, days or even weeks. They found the name and phone number of a sixty-six-year-old man in Susannah's diaries, and when traced and questioned the man could not explain why this should be so. He had never met this young woman called Susannah Lamplugh, he insisted, although he knew who she was from all the media publicity. There was absolutely no reason so far as he was concerned why Susannah should have his name in her book. He was mystified. Then he suddenly realized how it could have happened. Months before he had been selling his car through an advertisement in the local newspaper, and remembered receiving a call from a young woman who was interested in the car and had noted down his name and phone number. The call was never followed up. He could only surmise that the woman was the missing estate agent. The man's story stood up, and he was duly eliminated from the inquiries.

There were other coincidences almost too remarkable to be true. Detectives found out that Susannah had known a twenty-nine-year-old accountant called John Herring, who lived in Shorrolds Road – just fifteen doors from the house that she had apparently been showing to 'Mr Kipper'. He not only knew Susannah but owned a BMW too. Then it emerged that Herring's brother Peter was a client of Sturgis who had been on their mailing lists – and that John Herring was known to friends as 'Kip' or 'Kipper'. Such discoveries led to flurries of excitement in the incident room, but invariably came to nothing. Both the Herrings, like so many others, were quickly ruled out of any possible involvement with Susannah's disappearance. It was just another of the frustrating and surprising coincidences which seemed peculiarly common in this case.

Then they found out about a young BBC journalist called Leslie Skipper, who also knew Susannah. But he too was quickly eliminated. So was a Greek doctor called Kypros. People sent cuttings in: did the police know that a well-known Fleet Street cartoonist was named Kipper? That the husband of Bette Midler, the American entertainer, was known as 'Kipper'? That 'Mr Kipper' was cockney rhyming slang for Jack the Ripper? The file labelled 'Kipper Lookalikes' grew accordingly every day. Each time *Crimewatch* was shown, even long after the edition featuring Susannah Lamplugh, piles of such letters would come in. A boat was stolen from the beach in front of the Lamplughs' family holiday home in Wales – and the name of the boat happened to be 'Kipper'. But, excited though the mediums were by such news, there was no connection with Susannah Lamplugh's disappearance. The boat was later recovered, and the owner traced, interviewed and eliminated.

The hunt for the mystery married man, the one with whom

Susannah might have been having an affair, continued. Jon Hall, one of her boyfriends on the *QE*2, remembered that as they were making arrangements for the wedding they attended together shortly before she disappeared, Susannah had mentioned that she was seeing a married man. He had told her that she was asking for trouble, but Susannah did not seem concerned. The man was 'lovely', she told him. Later, when they were travelling up the M1 together in her office car to the wedding, he asked her again about the relationship – but this time she did not seem to want to talk about it. The man would not leave his wife, Susannah told Hall. There might have been a mention of children too, Hall vaguely recalled. But then the subject was dropped, and never came up again with Hall over the weekend.

No married men had come forward to volunteer that they were having a relationship with Susannah. What the detectives did not know was whether there had been more than one married man in Susannah's life, for several people who knew her had suggested there was such a man at different times in her life. Were they all referring to the same man or could there have been more than one? She had mentioned a married man to Hall less than five weeks before she went missing. Had she had a clandestine relationship with the same married man for two or three years? Had this man perhaps sent a bunch of flowers to Susannah that had mysteriously arrived one morning at the Sturgis office, with no note to say who they were from? There had been unexplained flowers delivered to her flat, too, the police recalled.

A woman estate agent then came forward to tell how she had been pestered by a local property speculator who had dealings with most of the local estate agents. She said the man had told her, in the midst of trying to impress her with his chatter, that before she went missing Susannah Lamplugh had been 'much more fun' than she was. Susannah had been to Stringfellows night club with him after they had completed a deal on property in Stevenage Road, he told the woman. He added that his cousin, who had accompanied them, was 'lucky' with Susannah that night. Because of the Stevenage Road connection, it sounded an interesting lead and the man and his alibis were thoroughly checked. He clearly had known and been attracted to Susannah, the investigations showed, but the matter had stopped there. The stories he told the other young estate agent about this relationship with Susannah seemed to be fantasy. Again, optimism in the incident room soon turned out to be temporary and baseless.

But before long there was another surprise. Elizabeth, Susannah's teenage sister now at Cheltenham College, remembered that Susannah had told *her* about a married man too. The man's name was possibly Mark or Alan, she told detectives. He was definitely rich and maybe aged twenty-nine or thirty. Three weeks before she had disappeared Susannah had asked Elizabeth at a swimming gala if she could borrow some of her youthful 'Sloaney' clothes, because she wanted to impress this man. Then, just before Elizabeth had left on her trip to Australia, New Zealand and Hong Kong – and just nine days prior to Susannah's disappearance – Susannah told her sister that the man was either married or about to get married. She stressed that what she told Elizabeth was a secret between them which was not to be told to their mother. Elizabeth thought that her sister told her mother only what she wanted her to hear.

The detectives went over all the possibilities again and again: the routes Susannah could have taken that day, the men she could have met, what could have happened after her appointment with 'Mr Kipper', always assuming that she *did* fulfil the 12.45 appointment and that it *was* a genuine one in the first place. It still did not make sense that Susannah's car should have been parked in Stevenage Road minutes after she left her office. The information was conflicting and the mystery was deepening all the time rather than becoming clearer. And what could be made of the evidence of Barbara Whitfield, the young woman who knew Susannah and swore that she had seen her with a young man in her car at 2.45 that afternoon? The detectives were by now divided about her evidence. Though investigations revealed that Barbara Whitfield had made her journey at the time she said she had made it, some were now convinced that she had been mistaken about seeing Susannah. Was she like the bookshop manageress, a decent and honest witness who had nevertheless become confused about what she had seen?

Whichever way they turned, the police inevitably came back to Sturgis and Susannah Lamplugh's work there. Mark Gurdon, the manager of the branch where Susannah worked, was carefully questioned about the movements of all the Sturgis staff on the day she disappeared. He himself had had lunch at the Crocodile Tears with two colleagues who worked at other Sturgis branches, he told them. He went carefully over the sequence of events that day: how he had first become concerned at about 3.30 that Susannah had not returned from her appointment, how he had hurried to 37 Shorrolds Road and then phoned hospitals to see if there had been an accident, and finally how he had reported Susannah missing to the police. Neither he nor any of the other employees had had an intimate relationship with Susannah, he added.

Inevitably, detectives checked discreetly with Gurdon's Sturgis colleagues who confirmed that he had indeed had lunch with them that day. When viewers of *Crimewatch* phoned to say that Gurdon looked similar to the photofit picture of 'Mr Kipper', the detectives merely laughed. They also routinely interviewed Martin Sturgis, the thirty-six-year-old senior partner in the family business. He had known Susannah, but the day she disappeared he was having lunch with his father at Langan's Brasserie in central London. Though Susannah was good friends with her Sturgis colleagues, it seemed that she was careful to avoid getting too close to them. However long the detectives talked to the Sturgis employees, it seemed they did not hold the key to Susannah's disappearance. The gradual elimination of all the clients did not give much cause for hope either.

But Diana Lamplugh, back in East Sheen Avenue, was developing another plan both to commemorate her daughter and help her family. The family would hold a service for Susannah in the local church where she had been a chorister. It would not be a funeral or even a memorial service, but a *celebration* of Susannah's life. Like her plans for The Suzy Lamplugh Trust, this idea did not at first win universal acclaim from those who had known Susannah well. Tamsin, still preferring to believe that her sister was alive and would come back to them, told her mother that it was far too early to hold such a service or even to think about one. But by the end of the fourth month, preparations were firm. The service would be held on 1 March – St David's Day. The church would be filled with daffodils and the sound of Welsh hymns, but would not be too religious because 'the kids' would not like it. If Susannah returned, the service would still go ahead. But it would then become a thanksgiving.

The Suzy Lamplugh Trust, too, was fast becoming reality. The initial idea had come from Tim Battle, a businessman and family friend whose children had grown up with the Lamplughs'. He had been on holiday in Spain when his daughter ran up with the English newspapers reporting Susannah's disappearance. The shock stayed with him, and the following month he and his wife took Paul and Diana Lamplugh out to dinner. Battle clearly recognized their need to build something positive from such a tragedy, some lasting memorial that would help to make sense out of Susannah's disappearance. He suggested at first a 'Band Aid' project to help the relatives of victims of murders or abductions. Instead, The Suzy Lamplugh Trust had gradually taken shape.

The newly converted top floor of the Lamplughs' house was earmarked for its offices. Before long two secretaries would be taken on. The Trust was registered as a charity, and contributions from well-wishers were sent to East Sheen Avenue. A slogan was adapted from T. S. Eliot: 'From the end there is a beginning.' Help was given from *Elle* magazine, a fashion journal that Rupert Murdoch had acquired not long before. Ogilvy and Mather, a major public relations and advertising firm, was appointed to monitor press cuttings for the Trust. Reebok, the sportswear manufacturers, prepared a booklet entitled *Safe Running Guide* with a foreword by Diana Lamplugh. The objects of the Trust, as declared under the 1960 Charities Act, were:

(i) The preservation and protection of mental and physical health and in particular by the provision of counselling and support to the parents and families of females who have disappeared without trace or suffered injury, distress or death.

(ii) To promote research into the ways which females may fulfil their potential safely and satisfactorily within modern society and in particular with regard to their employment.

131

With considerable media coverage and with much public relations aplomb, The Suzy Lamplugh Trust was launched at the Law Society 128 days after Susannah disappeared. Six television crews covered the event, alongside radio reporters, magazine writers and newspaper journalists. The Trust's reported aim was to raise £450,000, and educate not just women but men as well about their safety at work. Diana Lamplugh explained that her daughter had ignored several simple safety rules on the day she went missing: 'She should have asked "Mr Kipper" to come to the office rather than meet him at the house. Having gone to the house with him, she should have let him inside the flat first and left the front door open so that she had a means of escape.' There was a poignant personal note which reminded everyone of the human toll of the tragedy: 'We've stopped listening for the phone,' she said. 'I no longer wait for that call.'

There was considerable goodwill towards The Suzy Lamplugh Trust, for the circumstances surrounding it were so tragic. Mrs Lamplugh said she wanted the fund-raising activities of the Trust to be fun, to reflect Susannah's attitudes to life: windsurfing events, parties, jogging, and so forth. Not everyone was clear about the purpose of the Trust, and her daughter Tamsin was among them; months later, she said she was still not sure why it had been established. But by this time Battle and his small executive committee (including the Lamplughs and Mary Asprey) had carefully researched the subject and were confident that they had almost coincidentally come across a widespread problem that needed attention: that of people's safety while they were going about their daily work. They wondered why no one had fully addressed the problems before, and felt there was a definite need for a single organiz-ation to research the subject and help and advise those affected.

Diana Lamplugh defined the purpose of the Trust at the media launch: 'When Suzy made that routine call on a Monday lunchtime in July last year, purely acting in her role as negotiator, it seems she was off guard and did not sense her vulnerability,' read her statement to a regional newspaper. 'An awareness of potential danger, a healthy respect for the male, his actions and reactions, might have helped to prevent her fall into an obvious trap. Suzy's abduction has brought to the surface a realization of the often unwitting hazards and dangers faced by the increasingly adventurous, ambitious and skilled women setting out with determination to conquer many new fields in today's world. In my experience women want to be able to work on an equal basis with their male colleagues, but to do so they need to be equipped with an awareness and knowledge of how to survive.'

Launching the Trust brought with it a blur of media interviews for Mrs Lamplugh – from *Woman's Hour* to *Pete Murray's Phone-In* to TV-am, *The Observer* to *Midweek* to Radio One, *Woman* to *The Independent* to *Time Out*, *The Scottish Daily Record* to the *Surrey Comet* to 'A Life in the Day' with *The Sunday Times Magazine*. To her amazement, she said in a letter to her brother that week, she was enjoying all the media interviews and found she could do them well too. For some reason, she added, she seemed to be able to relax and think while she was sitting beside the interviewer or presenter – and although it was proving expensive she had found 'an easy and effective way of dressing which is distinctive and not showy'. Her appearances, she added, were giving the Trust a very high profile.

Towards the end of the week the TV-am coverage on the morning of the launch showed to what extent Diana Lamplugh had become a media personality in less than five months. The report began with film of her receiving breakfast in bed at home, and went on to show her teaching swimming to her classes. Then she was interviewed about Susannah. She did not really have any hope that her daughter would now be found, she said to the TV-am interviewer. Next day she went further, telling a senior journalist from *The People* that she not only believed Susannah was dead but also suggesting that she knew the identity of her killer: 'I can't say more or give details because that would be libellous ... Who gains by Suzie's disappearance? I don't, because I've lost a daughter. The kids don't, they've lost a sister. But there are people who stand to gain. I have my theory. I think Suzie has been killed. I think I know why the car was parked in Stevenage Road, but I'd rather not say ... Well, think about it. Use your logic. This is the area you should investigate.'

Though Mrs Lamplugh had in private named men whom she thought should be considered as suspects, the police had by this time eliminated all the people she felt should be targets in the investigation. But the combination of the information coming in from the police with the often contradictory outpourings of the sundry mediums and clairvoyants could only bring confusion. Shortly before the launch of The Suzy Lamplugh Trust, a woman Diana Lamplugh called the 'Queen Medium' visited East Sheen. She was dressed from top to toe in brilliant red, and wore a scarlet floor-length coat with scarlet breeches and boots. She said she was interested in Susannah's work at Sturgis and the 'war games' weekend she had been to with a friend. And then came her advice: the Lamplughs should now hire a private detective if they wished to find their daughter. They took the advice seriously and spent a disturbed night worrying about whether they should. In the event, they decided to leave the investigation in the hands of the police.

But increasingly they were relinquishing any hope that Susannah would be found. Just as Christmas was approaching, Diana Lamplugh became depressed because she feared that her daughter was no longer news and that the case would be forgotten. The family considered going to Mrs Lamplugh's brother in the United States for Christmas, but decided Susannah would have wanted them to have their normal family Christmas at home. Nevertheless they found that people treated them differently because of what had happened to them. Christmas cards to them seemed to have been chosen carefully and were often handed over diffidently, as though friends did not now know quite how to react to the Lamplughs. They received none of their usual invitations to parties, so decided to organize their own.

What then happened showed just how much the Lamplughs' way of life had changed since the disappearance of Susannah. For this Christmas, a television crew filmed Paul and Tamsin Lamplugh as they put cards on their mantelpiece at East Sheen Avenue, while Diana Lamplugh was shown working upstairs on The Suzy Lamplugh Trust. 'It's a job which simply must be done, and that gives one hope that something positive is coming out of it,' she told viewers. Then carol singers were filmed as they came into the house, and Diana Lamplugh was shown serving them mince pies and hot punch. The television item came out really well, Mrs Lamplugh told a friend later.

Buying Christmas presents turned out not to be a problem, and the family tried to keep to a normal routine, for example by taking Elizabeth to Harrods on Christmas Eve. They went to midnight communion, when Paul Lamplugh's eyes filled with tears. But his son Richard helped him by saying they all had to pull through, for one another's sake. They opened their presents on Christmas morning in the newly decorated bedroom, and then walked again to the local church. This time Tamsin wept quietly, for the absence of her sister was palpable. Christmas lunch for the family was at the house Tamsin now shared with Michael Hough, one of Susannah's former boyfriends, where they enjoyed champagne, smoked salmon and a Harrods' Christmas pudding; traditionally Susannah had made the family's Christmas puddings. Relatives phoned them during the day to keep up their morale. But throughout there was what Diana Lamplugh described as a 'huge emptiness' where their eldest daughter should have been. They went to Wales for the New Year, and it was just as bad.

By now the family were nevertheless celebrities. The Suzy Lamplugh Trust had already become a nationally known institution. But of Susannah Lamplugh herself, the unwitting cause of this extraordinary phenomenon, there was no news at all. The police had already warned the Lamplughs that although they would continue to follow up any leads, they would soon have no choice but to run down the investigation. The number of detectives on the case would be reduced to a handful. Because of this news the Lamplughs once again consulted Sir David Napley, the eminent solicitor who had helped them in the early fraught days. He too agreed that the police had done everything they could, and there was nothing more to ask of them.

But within days the Lamplugh investigation would be dramatic front-page news across the nation once again. For what none of them knew was that a forty-eight-year-old London businessman had been doing his own detective work, and had come up with some fascinating news. He had spent the period before Christmas trying to trace the owner of a BMW that had been mysteriously abandoned months before near his home in St John's Wood, in the innocent hope that he could buy it himself. And then he found out that the car belonged to a Mr Kiper.

Chapter Ten

The Christmas and New Year holiday had been more difficult for the Lamplughs than they had expected. It brought with it that inevitable slowing down, a time for reflection and reassessment – and the brutal realization that Susannah was no longer a member of the family, and that their own lives had changed irrevocably too. Early in the new year Diana Lamplugh expressed her feelings in one of her letters: 'It also takes a lot of energy just to blugeon [*sic*] through the feelings of loss, guilt, fear, horror and grief about Suzy, the cruelty of its effect on the other kids and Paul, her friends, on all of us . . . and what is more we can see no end.' The loss was felt in so many small, unexpected ways. Myfanwy, the faithful Lamplugh family cat, had reached the age of twenty and was so infirm that it seemed sensible that she should be put down. But because she was Susannah's cat, nobody could bear to make that decision.

The new year began unpromisingly in other ways. Detective Superintendent Carter, who was still formally heading the investigation, was on the verge of retiring to start a new life on a ten-acre smallholding in Somerset. He was regarded with almost universal affection by the policemen who worked under him as well as the civilians with whom he came into contact, and all concerned feared that as he departed so would a vital urgency to solve the case from within the police force. He had been personally involved from the beginning, even helping to move the Lamplughs' furniture during their house renovations, and he did not want to retire from the police leaving the most celebrated case of his career unsolved.

But he effectively did so over the holiday, and later held an emotional farewell party at a night club in Southall for more than 300 people. The Lamplughs were invited, and Diana and Tamsin Lamplugh proved to be among only a handful of women present. Later Paul Lamplugh made an impromptu speech of thanks to Carter, and policemen told the family afterwards that it was so rare to be thanked for what they did for the victims of crimes. With a shepherd's crook that was presented to him, the now plain Mr Nick Carter then left for the country. It was the end of an era.

But just when morale was dragging both with the Lamplughs and the police, there suddenly seemed to be an unaccountable new momentum. Even the mediums and clairvoyants started coming up with new ideas and theories, and Diana Lamplugh discovered that she had given them the wrong time of Susannah's birth all along. She had thought her first daughter was born shortly after *The Archers* on the wireless, but then found that the birth had actually been later and that the correct time was 8.20 p.m. That made all the difference to the mediums, who now apparently had to start entirely reconsidering the way they had been looking at Susannah's disappearance. Before long, Mary Asprey organized them on digs in areas of the country as far apart as Sussex and Buckinghamshire, but they found nothing.

In the early days of the new year Paul Lamplugh, too, provided a new impetus to the investigation. He recalled that Susannah had said casually to him one day that a client had offered to put up the money for a house or flat for her. When the police heard this they considered it a piece of possibly crucial information. Was 'Mr Kipper' a Sturgis client after all? Just when the theory had been losing ground, it started to gain more support from the investigating team – and the backgrounds of more than two hundred Sturgis clients were re-examined with renewed vigour. But the real breakthrough, or so it seemed at the time, came just three days into the new year.

It had all started innocently enough. Back in August Richard Ward, a businessman living in north London, was taking his dog for a walk when he first noticed a car abandoned in Queen's Grove, St John's Wood. It did not move for weeks, and when autumn turned into winter Ward started wondering how such a car could be left unclaimed for so long – for it was an expensive, metallic-blue two-litre BMW 518. Surely someone would miss such a car? The explanation, he presumed, was that the car was stolen. It had Belgian number plates, which probably meant that because it involved complicated procedures the British police had not traced the owner or alerted the Belgian authorities to ask them to do so. The Belgian driver, Ward reasoned, almost certainly had no idea that his car was languishing and slowly rotting on a north London street.

In the coming weeks the abandoned car became almost an obsession with Ward. It had already been broken into, a window broken and a stereo radio and cassette player stolen. Ward vowed that if the police took no action he would do something about the car himself, and might even try to buy it. His first step was to try to trace the Belgian owner, using the Automobile Association in Belgium. The owner, the information soon came back, was a David Kiper apparently living in Antwerp. In December Ward went to Belgium and tried to locate Kiper there – but with no success. Then, back in England, the realization hit him. In Flemish 'Kiper' sounded something like 'Kipper'. The man wanted in connection with the missing estate agent Suzy Lamplugh was a 'Mr Kipper', he recalled, and there were reports of a blue BMW being involved too. Had he unwittingly solved one of the great mysteries of the time? He went straight to the Lamplugh squad with his information.

By this time the detectives were used to plausible false alarms, for the Lamplugh investigation seemed to have more than its fair share of them. But in this case so much of the information seemed to fit, and they swiftly began to take an interest – the first step being to ask Belgian colleagues for more information. The car had been reported stolen, Brussels police replied, in the seaside resort of Knokke-Heist on 20 September. The registered owner was David Kiper, apparently an Israeli citizen who had nevertheless given an address in Antwerp. But the owner of the car, they said, was actually a thirty-three-year-old diamond dealer of the same address named David Rosengarten. His mother's maiden name was Kiper. Rosengarten apparently sometimes used the name himself, but they had ascertained that David Kiper was actually a separate person, an elderly Israeli uncle. Rosengarten himself lived in the Jewish quarter of Antwerp, but also spent time in Hong Kong, Israel and the United States. And a Belgian detective, in the words of a London counterpart, thought that he was 'a dead ringer' for the identikit picture of 'Mr Kipper'.

It was suddenly all very exciting for the Lamplugh squad. Why was the car reported stolen only on 20 September when it was definitely abandoned in London weeks before? Why in a seaside resort? Why had the owner apparently made no real effort to trace it? And why all this confusion over the names? Detective Inspector Johnstone and Detective Sergeant Barley decided they would have to make some inquiries across the Channel, and told the Lamplughs in confidence that they might at long last be on to something. Perhaps the long investigation into the disappearance of Susannah Lamplugh would soon be over.

But it was going to take a lot of work. A very complex procedure had to be followed before British detectives could work in a foreign country – both in Britain and then in the country concerned. The Lamplugh team had first to present their reasons for wanting to go to Belgium to a senior Metropolitan Police officer, in this case an assistant commissioner. Following his approval they had to apply for what is still known in Britain as a *commission rogatoire*, an internationally agreed form of formal communication between the police forces of two countries requesting co-operation from one of them. That could be issued in Britain by only one man, the Crown Prosecutor. So the right pieces of paper were put before him, and he duly issued the *commission rogatoire*.

All the documents outlining why the London detectives were interested in interviewing Kiper had then to be translated and telexed through Interpol to Brussels. But the reply almost immediately came back from Belgian police: 'This is in French, and we need to have it in our official language, Flemish.' There followed a frantic search in London for someone who could translate from English into Flemish, and a man was soon located in Wallington. The documents were rushed to him, and after he had translated them the results were telexed again, through Interpol, to Belgium. This time they were put before the Belgian King's Prosecutor, who had to decide whether the British police had a reasonable case for wanting to interview a Belgian suspect on Belgian soil. His decision was soon flashed to the incident room in Kensington. Yes, the British police had a case and could come to Belgium to pursue their man.

But two problems had arisen meanwhile. The first was that in the early days of 1987 Britain and Europe were enduring their worst winter cold spell for years, and Johnstone was marooned by snowdrifts in his village in Surrey. He was unable to drive to London or anywhere else, yet because he (with Barley) knew more about the case than any of the other detectives he was clearly the man to interrogate Rosengarten. The *commission rogatoire*, in any case, specified the two named men, and only them, as the detectives who would go to Belgium. The second problem was that the Kiper development had leaked to the press, who were becoming very agitated and practically accusing Rosengarten of Susannah's abduction. Independent Television News were the first to break the story, and the Lamplughs were suddenly beseiged by more reporters. Over the phone Richard Lamplugh warned his mother not to become excited, but she was unable to help it and phoned Tamsin and Adam Leegood, one of Susannah's boyfriends. The case of Susannah Lamplugh was once again on the front page of every newspaper in the country.

The problem for the detectives was that they had to be seen to be doing something. With the press baying at their heels, they felt they had no choice but to leave for Belgium immediately. But how? The Metropolitan Police moves swiftly in such cases. In his Surrey house Johnstone received a phone call telling him a police helicopter would be flying in to pick him up in five minutes. Surrealistically, Johnstone found himself whirring over the snow-covered Surrey hills to London's heliport in Battersea. Barley was waiting for him there. Then they were both flown by helicopter to Gatwick for a conventional airline flight to Belgium. They arrived at Gatwick breathless and with minutes to spare, only to see the crime correspondent of *The Standard* grinning contentedly at them in the departures lounge. He had driven furiously through the snow from his office in London, and had beaten them to it.

Seeing the journalist waiting for them at the airport gave the two detectives a foretaste of what was to come. The Lamplugh case was still urgent news that intrigued a nation. By the time Johnstone and Barley reached their hotel in Antwerp, they realized the British media would be coming in force too. By the second day reporters were in the bars, foyers, waiting outside their rooms in corridors – and the two policemen, hoping to make delicate inquiries in a foreign country, found they could not move for the British media. The reporters were already sending back sensational stories to Britain, too. 'SUZY riddle of the BMW' was the typical front-page splash in *Today*. 'Kiper story doesn't add up, say Police.' It was all getting out of control.

Yet they could not just swoop in and arrest Rosengarten. That was not correct police procedure in any case: any detective knew that before interviewing a suspect he should amass as much intelligence on him as possible for ammunition during the interrogation. But Johnstone and Barley realized they still had no powers at all in Belgium. They could do nothing without the help of the Belgian police, and before that was forthcoming they had themselves to appear personally before the King's Prosecutor and formally present their *commission rogatoire*. Then, and only then, could they start doing the job. A Belgian detective was appointed by the King's Prosecutor to help the two British policemen.

The Lamplughs, meanwhile, were busy talking to the media in Britain. Two new theories linking the Belgian suspect with Susannah Lamplugh had emerged in the press while Johnstone and Barley were in Antwerp. The first suggested link went back to Susannah's skiing holiday in Val-d'Isère the previous March: one of Rosengarten's hobbies, it had been reported from Belgium, was skiing. Dave Hodgkinson, one of her boyfriends on the trip, recalled that she had apparently met a French-speaking man on the slopes with whom she was very taken. Could this man, the speculation went, be Rosengarten?

The second theory came about because Rosengarten, a bachelor, had a flat in Hong Kong – a place Susannah had visited while she was working on the *QE2*. Had they met and formed a relationship then? Diana Lamplugh took a newspaper's photograph of Rosengarten - his face was now all over the British press – to show waitresses at Crocodile Tears, the wine bar in Fulham Road across from Susannah's Sturgis office. Yes, the waitresses replied. That man might *well* have been in the wine bar. If it was up to feeling in Britain, the Belgian diamond dealer would now have been standing trial for Susannah's abduction.

But the hapless Johnstone and Barley, still receiving their crash course in Belgian constitutional law, already knew that under Belgian law a national could not be extradited to Britain to face trial. The procedure was that he would face trial for any alleged offences in Britain in a Belgian court. They were still powerless in Belgium, and totally reliant on the co-operation of the Belgian police. If they were to interrogate Rosengarten, they learned, it would have to be through Belgian colleagues – and conducted in the Flemish language. Just to make their life even more complicated they were now unable to leave their hotel or even walk into the office of the police in Antwerp without being pursued desperately for information by the British media pack.

By now Rosengarten's life, too, was being made a misery. Armed police were guarding his sixth-floor flat. He became so incensed by the allegations and questions being shouted through his letter box by British journalists that he decided to go voluntarily to Antwerp police headquarters – and there, before they were properly prepared, Johnstone and Barley had to start their questioning of him through their Belgian counterparts. The questioning went on from late morning until early evening, and Rosengarten was by no means overly forthcoming about his life. He could not explain how the car came to be in London, why it was registered in the name of an elderly relative – or how often he came to London. But on one thing he was completely adamant: he did not know Susannah Lamplugh, had never met her and had no connection whatso-ever with her or her disappearance.

The photographs of Rosengarten being published in Britain actually looked only vaguely like 'Mr Kipper'. The Belgian's face was altogether plumper, and although only thirty-three he looked older. In short, he was clearly not Susannah's type of man, even though as an international diamond dealer he certainly did lead the glamorous and ritzy lifestyle to which she might be attracted.

There was another aspect of the story which the detectives now knew but which the media did not, and which made Rosengarten less convincing as a suspect. The BMW belonging to Rosengarten which had been abandoned in London was not the same model that Richard Turner had reported seeing in Shorrolds Road. He told police that the car he had seen the day Susannah disappeared was *similar* to a 518, but was at least ten years old – while Rosengarten's was a 1980s model. To this extent at least, the links between Susannah Lamplugh and David Rosengarten were more tenuous than ever. Forensic evidence taken from the abandoned BMW in London did not produce any connection with Susannah either. Now it was only the names 'Kiper' and 'Kipper' that seemed to link them.

Exactly what his car was doing in London was never estab-lished, or the circumstances in which it had disappeared.

But the London detectives soon realized as they talked to Rosengarten – occasionally in English, for he turned out to be fluent in the language – that this was proving to be another of the astonishing coincidences that had proved such an unusual part of the Lamplugh investigation. Rosengarten was able to produce a receipt from an Antwerp garage that showed his car was being serviced on Monday 28 July 1986 – the day Susannah disappeared. They checked its authenticity with the garage's computer records, and David Rosengarten, alias Mr Kiper, was totally in the clear. *He had no connections whatsoever with Susannah Lamplugh.* Six days after they went to Belgium with such high hopes, Johnstone and Barley flew home to Britain. Despite all the flurries of intense speculation that were still appearing in the British press they knew that their investigations were back to square one.

But the media zealots refused to give up. The *Sunday Express* flew Harry Riglin, the man who lived in Shorrolds Road and thought he had seen Susannah with 'Mr Kipper' outside number 37, to Antwerp to see if he could recognize Rosengarten. 'He is just like the mysterious Mr Kipper I saw with Suzy last July,' he was then quoted as saying. 'I came to Antwerp fully prepared to say "That's not the man." But now I have to admit it could be. Face to face, the similarity is amazing. He has the same boyish looks and build and he stands the same way.' Though the detectives knew without any doubt that Rosengarten was innocent, the press would not easily leave the story alone. They seemed to *want* poor Rosengarten to be guilty. Diana Lamplugh, in any case, was still keen to see the story of her missing daughter in the newspapers. That way, she described in a letter, pressure would be maintained on the police: 'Eventually we talked to the papers but of course by now they thought the car old hat so to try to "buy" their interest

I told them that we had now also got the "clue" that Daddy had remembered about Suzy saying that someone had offered to come in with her buying a flat and that she did seem to be looking at property beyond her means.'

The Antwerp case, it turned out, had stimulated the imaginations of those involved. If the man who had offered to put up money for Susannah was a diamond smuggler, Mrs Lamplugh now theorized, he might have needed a 'safe house' – hence the offer to Susannah. 'Of course the papers had a ball with this and went right over the top,' Mrs Lamplugh continued. 'I nearly went spare.' Then she received a phone call from a woman who suggested that Israeli intelligence was somehow involved in Susannah's abduction, and that started myriad new theories:

If it really did turn out to be connected in some way to someone say putting up the money to help Suzy buy a house (as we know they had offered) and that person was a member of a foreign intelligence service looking for a 'safe house' and that the Home Office or Special Branch had stopped the police search in Belgian [sic] (as it seemed they did) then it might turn out to be as big as Watergate! On the other hand this might all be in the realms of fantasy. At least when we look back on it we'll know we haven't left a stone unturned. Mary rang to tell me the 'mediums' now have a Private Detective going out to Portugal. Wonders will never cease!

Later Mrs Lamplugh phoned the *Sunday Express* to tell them about her new theory that Israeli intelligence was involved in her daughter's abduction. By now Diana Lamplugh's high profile in the media had made her a powerful figure, and she described a visit to the Home Office and her new way of life in a letter to her youngest daughter:

Then I asked them about our case – said I had been such a good advert for the Met that I really did not want to 'put the boot in' but wouldn't hesitate if I felt I needed to! They gave me a sympathetic hearing and I think I may well do something about it. Just to make sure I am going to see the Assistant Commissioner of the police tomorrow at Scotland Yard! I do hope Suzy knows what she puts me through. It seems to be one hurdle after another – but we keep surviving. The BBC were so narked that I hadn't called them first that they got a couple who lost their daughter seven years ago on Wogan! The Trust is growing in stature every day – the Baroness Young has become our Vice president and we are asked to approach our hopeful choice of Royal patron again. So keep your fingers crossed.

The plans for the service, meanwhile, were continuing apace. Susannah's brother Richard suggested that a Welsh choir be brought to London from Newport for the occasion – but that did not prove practical. The Lamplughs prepared 400 invitations to the service, though they did not expect everyone they invited to attend. The date was fixed firmly for 1 March – St David's Day – but they had still not decided exactly what form the service would take. A permanent memorial, though, was by now already built into the house at East Sheen Avenue: a round, stained-glass window which two friends had volunteered to make and which was erected in the wall by the front door. It featured depictions of sea and sky and land with a lily and daffodils, and the words 'Suzy Lamplugh – although absent her light still shines' and 'Suzy Lamplugh, aged 25, abducted without trace while at work . . .' It represented Susannah's love for the outdoors and the family were delighted with it. With spring approaching, her light was now shining into the house in East Sheen Avenue where she had grown up.

But the police investigation was fast running aground. Hopes had risen dramatically among the policemen and women while Rosengarten was a suspect, but now he had been cleared the detectives were once again reduced to following possible but unlikely leads. No suspicion could be attached to any of the known Sturgis clients, and there were no obvious suspects from the *QE*2 either. Those close to Susannah Lamplugh personally or professionally – Leegood, Hodgkinson, Bryant and Gurdon, for example – had been throughly investigated and eliminated. So had others in the Putney Set. Every scrap of information concerning sightings in Stevenage Road or Shorrolds Road had been pursued with an almost religious intensity. Countless alibi statements had been taken. The vast carousels of information expanded daily and Woman Detective Constable Harrison still patiently cross-indexed all the incoming information. But finding Susannah or her abductor now seemed further away than ever. Perhaps, a detective would occasionally wonder out loud, Susannah Lamplugh was still alive and really living it up in the Bahamas or some similar part of the world. No one was in a position to say otherwise with any certainty.

The other problem for the police was that while they had been hunting for Susannah, time had not stood still. Murders, rapes and serious robberies in west London had been continuing steadily since Susannah went missing, and all such cases had to be investigated too. The resources for criminal investigations in one of the busiest parts of inner-city London were finite. That meant that the pressure on the Lamplugh squad was mounting daily, for they were using valuable space in the incident room of AMIP (Area Major Investigation Police) headquarters in Kensington. A difficult and poignant decision could not be delayed any longer. The Lamplugh team and their carousels, the locked cupboards with Susannah's purse and diaries and lost cheque book and other essential exhibits in the case, would be moved to a rented building in Hammersmith already used by the detectives as an annexe. Though nobody acknowledged it publicly, the Lamplugh investigation was being discreetly downgraded.

But there was still one hopeful line of investigation left. Richard Turner, the car enthusiast who thought he had seen a BMW double-parked in Shorrolds Road at about the time Susannah disappeared, voluntarily contacted the police after conducting some research of his own. He was now satisfied, he told detectives, that the car he had seen was not a BMW 518 but a model from the 2000 series dating from the early 1970s. They were similar, but different. That new information narrowed down the number of targeted cars dramatially, and the detectives ran a check with the police national computer to find out how many such cars were still on the roads. There were 3,643 blue BMWs in the London area, it revealed, but only 278 blue BMW 2000s from that period.

Many of these had probably been scrapped by now, because the Driver and Vehicle Licensing Centre in Wales reported that they had not heard from a sizeable minority of the cars' owners for more than four years. But to locate and then interrogate all the drivers of even the remaining vehicles about their movements on a specific date the previous summer was still a major undertaking. For the senior police management, whether to proceed with this line of inquiry was an unenviable decision – for they knew that more mundane but equally serious cases had to be investigated and solved too, even though they would result in few if any headlines. Following much heart-searching, they decided that the chances of finding Susannah Lamplugh's abductor through interviewing BMW 2000 car owners and drivers was relatively small and did not justify the expenditure of such scarce time and resources.

The senior men of Scotland Yard had reckoned without Diana Lamplugh, though. The police hierarchy was now extremely wary of her, because her daughter's disappearance and her ensuing adeptness with the media had turned her into a powerful figure. If she pronounced herself dissatisfied with the police investigation – whether such a view was reasonable or not – they knew the result would be sensational headlines that they could do little to control. She had therefore become not just influential through the media, but was also now effectively in a position to tell police what she thought should be done in the investigation. And the police had to listen. So when Mrs Lamplugh phoned Scotland Yard and asked to speak to a Deputy Assistant Commissioner she had met at Carter's retirement party, she was put through immediately. She suggested, Diana Lamplugh recalled later, that it might be 'a good idea' if he saw her. He could hardly have had a higher rank in the force, but according to her own account needed little persuading to arrange a meeting.

Now Diana Lamplugh and her husband were discussing the case not just with the CID officers at Fulham police station – the detectives originally assigned to the case – but with one of the most senior officers in the country. She knew how high she was going, she said later, when she found herself facing a guard on the seventh floor of the New Scotland Yard building. She and the officer talked cordially for some time. 'By then he knew that I meant business and we got on very well,' she wrote in a newsletter. That evening, Mrs Lamplugh later reported, the phone rang in East Sheen Avenue and a Scotland Yard man told her that she need not go to the press. The detectives would now look at BMW 2000s all over the country, and not just in London or even Bristol (where Susannah's alleged married boyfriend might have lived) – and ten extra detectives would now be added to the team.

It was a notable victory for the Lamplughs, and an indication of how much influence they could now wield. Because of Mrs Lamplugh's determination, the police investigation was no longer running aground. The service for Susannah was set for St David's Day. The Suzy Lamplugh Trust would be officially dedicated then, but it was already achieving considerable publicity. The memorial window to Susannah was in place. Diana Lamplugh was being interviewed constantly by a curious media. Spring was coming.

Then, on Friday 13 February, Paul Lamplugh came home after his daily commuter walk from Mortlake station. His wife regaled him with news of her successes with the police. 'You've done really well,' he told her. But there was something about his manner that made Diana Lamplugh ask her husband about *his* day. His reply immediately alerted her to the realization that something serious had happened. 'He wants', Lamplugh told his wife in a peculiarly strained voice, 'to pay me off.' She knew straight away what he was saying. A new Secretary General had been in place at the Law Society for a fortnight and was already busily streamlining the bureaucracy. Now, she learned as her husband outlined the day's events, departmental secretaries aged fifty-five or over were being phased out. And Paul Lamplugh, less than seven months after his daughter had gone missing, was one of them. He had lost his job.

Chapter Eleven

There were very few hopes left for the detectives. Even the investigation into the BMW drivers, some of them were convinced, was a long shot that was very unlikely to yield any significant results. But because the case was continuing to receive so much publicity policemen at all levels still wanted to be the ones who would solve the baffling Suzy Lamplugh case. There were constant volunteers from within the police to examine the files. But Detective Superintendent Carter had left the force convinced that no angle had been left unexplored. Both Detective Inspector Johnstone and Detective Sergeant Barley, the men left with the daily running of the investigation, believed the same. But the nagging fear remained that they might have overlooked some obvious lead.

The investigation had come to dominate the private lives of the detectives. Barley and his fiancée – also a detective working on the Lamplugh investigation – made a firm rule that they would limit discussion of it in their free time to one hour a day. Others in the team were still lying awake at night mulling over all the possibilities about Susannah Lamplugh's movements that fateful day months before. Had she been to Stevenage Road? Shorrolds Road? Had she met 'Mr Kipper' there? Did she know the man she was apparently going to meet? How could all the contradictory evidence be explained? Despite all the hard work and the hundreds of thousands of man- and woman-hours spent on the case, there were still no definitive answers to any of these questions. Driving home one evening Johnstone was overtaken by a car with the registration plate

SUS 1E – and began to believe he had really been taken over by the case.

There always remained the possibility that they had become too close to the investigation, so after eight fruitless months it was decided that a completely fresh examination of the case needed to be made. A civilian unit in Scotland Yard existed for just this purpose, to look for loopholes in complex police investigations. It formed part of Scotland Yard's Criminal Intelligence Department known as SO11 and operated without publicity. The unit employed a study method known as the Anacapa system, named after the Californian island where it was developed. It was more usually used in long and involved fraud inquiries, in the hope that a new approach by people whose minds were uncluttered with theories and wrong assumptions would pinpoint some hitherto unexplored paths.

Two young members of this unit thus moved into the Lamplugh office in Hammersmith, full of hope that they might be able to solve the case. They had to read every statement, absorb every relevant detail in the investigation. Nothing could be ignored, for this might be where the police had gone wrong – if they had. Even the countless statements taken patiently by Scottish police, detailing how, for example, an old lady on a bus in Lothian was convinced 'Mr Kipper' had sat next to her that afternoon, had to be read carefully. Their method involved flow charts, visually depicting each stage of the investigation and in particular reconstructing the hours after Susannah went missing. The whereabouts of each man who had come under suspicion were depicted on the chart at the appropriate time. What witnesses had seen was similarly plotted. Events were taken forwards rather than backwards, which had been one of the main frustrations of the case. Before long the whole of one wall of the office in Hammersmith was taken up with the flow charts, and for weeks the team worked carefully looking for that crucial loophole.

But they never found one. Their own investigation merely confirmed that the Metropolitan Police inquiry into the disappearance of Susannah Lamplugh was as thorough as could be. There were no witnesses whose vital evidence had been ignored, no obvious suspect who had been missed, no deduction that had not been made or followed through. The presumed abduction remained a mystery. Though Johnstone and Barley never suspected otherwise, it was a welcome vindication of their hard work.

In another way it was also disappointing, for they wanted more than anything else to find Susannah Lamplugh and capture her abductor – if he existed. The Anacapa investigation merely led them back to their situation following Day One, with no definite clues, no real suspects, little useful evidence. Forensic experts had told them that the ecological changes of spring might expose a partly buried body, but there had been no such discovery. The extra police work following Diana Lamplugh's intervention had produced no significant new evidence. A detailed trawl of many drivers of BMW 2000s had only the familiar outcome: there was nothing to link any of them with Susannah Lamplugh. When the first anniversary of Susannah's disappearance came, some of the team vowed, that would be a suitable time to close down the investigation if no further clues presented themselves.

That thought depressed the Lamplughs. The news of Paul Lamplugh's forthcoming redundancy was the second trauma to afflict the family in just seven months and, like the first, came when it was least expected. The renovations in the East Sheen Avenue house were being carried out on the assumption that Lamplugh would continue to earn his salary. To find himself

without a salaried post in his mid-fifties was a grievous blow –
especially after he had been given a new job as Secretary to the
Ethics and Guidance Department of the Law Society so soon
after his daughter had disappeared. Because Susannah had
wished him well for the interview for that post at their last
meeting, the subsequent appointment was irrevocably
connected emotionally with the absent Susannah. Lamplugh
did know when he took up the post, however, that the whole
administrative structure of the Law Society might soon be
changed.

What had happened was that the management consultants
Coopers and Lybrand had made a thorough assessment of the
Law Society's structure in the months before Susannah went
missing. They had then delivered a report recommending
major changes in the managerial structure of the Society. A
new Secretary General later took over and swiftly implemented
many of Coopers and Lybrand's recommendations. Lamplugh
became one of four departmental secretaries over fifty-four
who were offered early retirement, with the work of his
department being absorbed into a new Professional Standards
and Development Directorate. A new head for that department
was sought from outside. The changes, the Law Society said,
were no reflection on Lamplugh's ability or performance and
they offered him consultancy work combined with compen-
sation and pension benefits. He would, in any case, work full-
time for the Society for another year.

But that did not change the impact of the news in East Sheen
Avenue. It was horrifying for Diana Lamplugh, who had
thought that her husband was working very successfully at the
Law Society. He was making a distinguished contribution to
the future of his profession, she felt. 'We feel hit on the head,
below the belt, and anywhere else you can think of and ours

[*sic*] will not be in private, the media are already on our trail . . .'
wrote Diana Lamplugh to her brother. 'And once more we will
have to brave it out, fight back, survive – just before the Service
on Sunday. No doubt it must be good for our soul!'

Faced with such news it was consoling that the service to
celebrate Susannah's life was now imminent. The organist and
choirmaster of All Saints Church in East Sheen invited the
Lamplughs for a drink to discuss the service just after they had
received the news of Lamplugh's redundancy, and proceeded
to read from a book called *The Prophet* by a Lebanese philos-
opher and poet, Kahlil Gibran. Suddenly it all fell into place
for the Lamplughs. Gibran had been dead for more than half
a century but his work had become fashionable on British
and North American campuses much more recently. To the
Lamplughs his words seemed to convey what they wanted to
say about their daughter. It was vigorous, lively and easily
understandable language that somehow avoided being ecclesi-
astically oppressive.

By this time Paul Lamplugh was too preoccupied to work on
the service, but when she returned home Diana Lamplugh
proceeded to cull extracts from the book. She then assigned
them to various individuals to read out in church: to friends
and lovers like Hough, Hodgkinson, Leegood and Doug
Williams. Sarah 'Puff' Hough was also given a reading. The
recently retired Detective Superintendent Carter was given a
section to read, as was Paul Lamplugh. Diana Lamplugh
herself and her children chose not to perform any readings
because their dyslexia meant that they sometimes had difficulty
reading out loud. But Barbara Murray, the actress, and the
actor Richard Briers were each given roles. The contribution
of the clergy was kept to a minimum, although the Reverend
Dr Colin Morris agreed to deliver the sermon. Diana Lam-

plugh sent scripts to all the the participants, and the church choir practised diligently.

The news of Paul Lamplugh's redundancy, meanwhile, had still not been made public. But then Diana Lamplugh discovered that the Law Society was planning to release news of its reorganization on the Friday before the service. The family had lived in the public eye since Susannah disappeared, and Mrs Lamplugh knew only too well that the press would want to make something of how her husband had lost his job. So she decided to take matters once again into her own hands. The news would be released not when the Law Society chose to release it, but when she wanted it released. She duly sprang the news on *The Standard*'s reporter Caroline Davies, who phoned the Law Society herself and then wrote a news story for her paper's late editions – the day before the news was due to be officially released. 'Suzy father is told: you've lost your job,' was the headline. The story was followed up in the newspapers next morning, the day the Law Society had planned to announce the news of its reorganization itself. The venerable old Law Society had been thwarted by Diana Lamplugh's instinctive feel for the media.

The service that followed was of profound symbolic importance for the Lamplughs. In so many obvious ways it fulfilled the cathartic role of a funeral, yet there was still demonstrable hope – and, above all, no coffin. By this time Tamsin, the elder of Susannah's two sisters, felt much more enthusiastic about the service. Diana Lamplugh wanted to hand every member of the congregation a daffodil bulb to plant, but instead settled for roses to be worn as buttonholes. Family friends filled the church with flowers, and a rehearsal for all the participants was held on the Saturday before. Friends of Susannah arranged for the service to be recorded on video, and the choirmaster set up sound recording equipment. The chosen day turned out to be ideal: a Sunday afternoon that marked, in Diana Lamplugh's words, the end of one phase and the beginning of another.

Three hundred attended the church, some of them patrons of the Trust who had not actually known Susannah herself but by now felt that they did. There were also friends both of Susannah and the family, Susannah's former headmistresses, her Guides captain, women who had had babies at the same time as Diana Lamplugh had had Susannah – sitting alongside police, journalists, even the 'Queen Medium' dressed again in bright red from head to toe. The Order of Service, with The Suzy Lamplugh Trust motif on the front and a Lamplugh coat of arms on the penultimate page, described the event as 'An Act of Healing in Celebration of the Life of Suzy Lamplugh and Dedication of The Suzy Lamplugh Trust.' There was a biography of Susannah, which described her as 'a much loved sparkling daughter and sister, a treasured friend and admired colleague'.

The vicar immediately set the tone at the beginning of the service: 'We are here to offer this celebration not knowing if she is dead or alive, only that she is not here – and in the confidence that good can come out of evil, and joy out of sorrow, through the Trust which bears her name, and in a thousand other ways.' The first hymn, to Parry's familiar Victorian tune 'Repton', was 'Dear Lord and Father of Mankind'. Then Paul Lamplugh gave the first reading from *The Prophet:*

> Your children are not your children.
> They are the sons and daughters of Life
> longing for itself.

> They come through you but not from you,
> And though they are with you they
>> belong not to you.

Following other similar readings and prayers Diana Lamplugh moved forward with the chairman of The Suzy Lamplugh Trust to present the deed of the Trust for a blessing by the Reverend Dr Morris. 'We dedicate the work of this Trust to the glory of God, to the service and protection of his children and to perpetuate the name of Suzy Lamplugh,' Morris pronounced. Then Paul Lamplugh spoke the first unscripted words of the service, which to many proved its most memorable part. First he thanked those who had helped with the service and those friends and relatives who had come to it – including the police, press and Mary Asprey, 'without whom none of us could have survived as we have'. Then he said the words which were to be so widely quoted afterwards: 'While we do not believe that Suzy is still alive, we also do not believe that she is dead. That is the paradox. But we must get on with our lives. We must live on positively, and that is the message of this service.'

Then Morris rose to speak, and his address continued for almost nine minutes. People reacted to human suffering in a number of ways, he told the congregation – often with dumb resignation, bitter anger or corrosive guilt. But the Lamplughs were not ordinary people and were turning their suffering to use it constructively and creatively. Jesus touched the lives of a small group of fishermen, and that group expanded. Now 'a happy south London girl' was touching the lives of a growing number of people too, so much so that it was 'amazing' the extraordinary range of people whose lives had been touched by her. Parsons and policemen, politicians and TV personalities, world champion karate experts and many others had been so touched. In one dimension the Lamplugh family had been sundered, but in another the whole family was now complete at the altar: 'No absent friends, no missing loved ones, all the family complete.' It was a moving address.

The point about the service, Mrs Lamplugh said later, was that it brought out everyone's happy memories of Susannah. Friends told her they felt much better for having come. Tamsin Lamplugh pronounced the service 'brilliant'. Her father thought it provided some kind of release. Diana Lamplugh was so pleased with Colin Morris's address that she asked Rabbi Julia Neuberger, who had become a patron of The Suzy Lamplugh Trust, to contribute similar thoughts from a Jewish perspective for the Trust's magazine (which she later did). The family and friends went on afterwards to the White Lodge in Richmond Park, where they had what Mrs Lamplugh described as a 'sumptious [*sic*] tea' provided by the Royal Ballet School. Then some friends returned to East Sheen Avenue for a drink, and by this time the Lamplughs were ready to sleep after another emotionally exhausting but strangely fulfilling day. It had been an uplifting, sad, joyous time.

For the policemen who had attended the service there was to be no rest. Detective Inspector Johnstone and Detective Sergeant Barley headed straight back to the headquarters of the investigation in Hammersmith, still determined to solve the mystery. The service was on a Sunday, but by now they were used to giving up their own time on the case. Both the detailed Anacapa check and the partial investigation of BMW 2000 drivers had proved fruitless, but there was still one last hopeful line of inquiry. A year after Susannah disappeared, they would return to all the key witnesses and suspects to see if anything fresh had come to their minds. In particular what interested them was the party given in Surrey by the young estate agent friend of Susannah on the Saturday before she went missing. Had members of the Putney Set who were there that evening missed any vital clues?

There was also another motive. Few people can commit a murder and then not give at last some psychological hints to those around them about what they have done. The detectives wanted to look for any obvious changes in the personalities of Susannah's friends, colleagues, clients or lovers over the previous year. Had any turned to drink or drugs? Or experienced any kind of nervous breakdown? Any unusual behaviour in the people previously interviewed would interest them, though the inquiries had to be discreet and not upsetting for those involved.

The dramatic false alarms continued meanwhile. A senior detective came into the office one morning to be told that a member of the public had just phoned the team to say that skeletal bones had been found in a garden close to the Sturgis office in Fulham Road. The detective asked the name of the householder in whose garden the remains had been found and walked over to the revolving carousel containing thousands of names. He looked for the man's name on the index cards just in case it happened to be there – and to his astonishment it was. *And* the man had known Susannah Lamplugh, *and* he was a former client of the Fulham Road Sturgis office. There was yet another flurry of intense excitement in the office, and the bones were rushed to a hospital mortuary for examination. The pathologist's report was flashed back: though they seemed at first glance to be, the remains were not human. The umpteenth possible suspect was cleared almost as soon as he had joined the ranks of suspects.

There then followed one curious development which was

never satisfactorily explained. Kenneth Heminsley, the former acting landlord of the Prince of Wales public house in Upper Richmond Road – who had discovered Susannah's missing cheque book, pocket diary and a postcard on the front steps of his pub late on the Friday evening before she went missing – talked to the police again and this time seemed to come up with some new information. Like most, if not all, the other witnesses in the case, he was a patently honest and straightforward person. He was now thirty, and had returned to live in the north of England. Susannah Lamplugh had arranged to pick up her lost belongings at six o'clock the day she went missing, he recalled. That afternoon, he now told police, someone who said her name was Sarah had telephoned him and left a message for Susannah (apparently for when she turned up at the pub) to ring her at a number which he wrote down. Some time later a man also spoke to him on the phone, saying he was a policeman.

The detectives to whom he told all this were aghast, for they knew no policeman could have phoned Heminsley on the afternoon Susannah went missing – well before the disappearance had even been reported to the police. He was adamant, too, that he had given the scrap of paper on which he had written the name and phone number to the police when he was originally interviewed a day or so later. But the squad certainly had no such piece of paper, which could possibly have been of immense importance. Neither could they trace Sarah, for she certainly was not Sarah 'Puff' Hough, Susannah's friend, or any other traceable Sarah she had known. Was the call actually made by Susannah herself, possibly under duress from 'Mr Kipper'? Was it a plea for help? Was the 'policeman' who Heminsley said phoned him really the abductor himself? It was all very baffling, especially as the two detective constables who had first interviewed Heminsley (soon after Susannah went missing) strongly insisted that they were not given any such piece of paper. The two men were valued and trusted members of the investigative team, and finally the senior detectives concluded that, again as in the case of so many others, Heminsley's memory was playing tricks. But it left an uneasy feeling.

Letters and phone calls with apparently important information continued to flood into the inquiry office too. Women estate agents were propositioned or attacked every day somewhere in the country, it seemed, and invariably local police would inform the Lamplugh squad. But equally invariably, the attacks would prove to have no connection with Susannah Lamplugh. A teenage estate agent in Pimlico, just along the Thames from Fulham, claimed to have been attacked and raped by a client but she did not want to press charges. The squad looked into it but soon ruled the suspect out. A detective received a letter from a prisoner who, months before, he had helped to convict in court: 'I have vital evidence about Suzy Lamplugh, the missing estate agent. You must come here [to HM prison] and I will tell you about it. Please don't forget to bring some family-sized SIGNAL toothpaste when you come.' It was, they decided, only a ruse to acquire some toothpaste he apparently coveted. A considerable part of the work of the team was to separate the hoaxes from the real leads.

This continuing police work helped the Lamplughs to feel that all that could be done to find their daughter was still being done. The shock of Paul Lamplugh's unexpected redundancy gradually lessened and prospects seemed not to be as bad as they had been. The Law Society proposed to keep him on the payroll as a 'consultant' even after the year he had remaining on the staff. 'They know now they have made a terrible mistake but of course they cannot go back and lose face,' his wife wrote in a newsletter. The two Lamplugh daughters flew to Switzerland for a holiday, and then the family went to Wales again for Easter. It was ideal Lamplugh weather: warmth and sun combined with wind for surfing and sailing. The usual houseful of people surrounded the family, with young friends of both Susannah and Tamsin coming as usual too. Less than a fortnight later the family returned to Wales for what would have been Susannah's twenty-sixth birthday. Diana Lamplugh found she had gained half a stone in weight – after a year it was a full stone – while her daughter Tamsin actually lost weight following a severe throat infection.

Their lives were also changing because of the way The Suzy Lamplugh Trust was developing. Diana Lamplugh in particular threw her considerable charm, energy and devotion into speaking at meetings across the country about safety at work and related matters, broadcasting on radio and television, and arranging a hectic future for the Trust. Baroness Young, a respected member of Mrs Thatcher's government, agreed to become its Vice-President ('we are saving the top for Royalty!' Mrs Lamplugh confided in another newsletter).

Soon Diana Lamplugh herself was also in demand as a speaker, and found they sometimes brought in donations of £100 or more. A publisher arranged an advance of £10,000 for a book on safety at work. A trading company was set up, with Paul Lamplugh as secretary and Mary Asprey as director, called Suzy Lamplugh Ventures Ltd. (The mechanics of establishing the company actually involved acquiring another firm called Soapmere Ltd which dealt in fancy goods and antiques. Later they changed its name, and Baroness Ewart-Biggs and the other trustees became shareholders.) A firm started marketing Suzy Lamplugh Alarms. Filofax expressed an interest in producing Suzy Lamplugh Packs. A video was made by the Citizens' Advice Bureau, with sponsorship from the employment agency Kelly Girl Services Ltd and the Royal Institution of Chartered Surveyors. The new top-floor office in the Lamplugh household in East Sheen Avenue started to buzz with activity. Fees from broadcasting and royalties from books – including 50p for every Suzy Lamplugh Alarm sold – would go to the The Suzy Lamplugh Trust.

Diana Lamplugh also started a campaign to require the registration of mini-cabs, a subject the police had told her about. By now Diana Lamplugh had become a much more powerful and influential figure than the swimming and Slimnastics teacher she had been before her daughter's disappearance. Six members of Parliament had become patrons of The Suzy Lamplugh Trust, and now she was able to discuss issues with any of them when she chose to do so. If she wanted to talk to Douglas Hurd, not only the Home Secretary but also the member of the Cabinet ultimately in charge of the Metropolitan Police, he was only a phone call away.

For the mini-cabs campaign she went first to see Jo Richardson, Labour MP for Barking and a veteran civil rights and nuclear disarmament campaigner. 'She was of course very enthusiastic,' Mrs Lamplugh said later. She discussed the subject too with her local Conservative MP, Jeremy Hanley. Following a talk on mini-cabs in Putney, she was invited to see David Mellor, then a junior minister in the Home Office and one of the rising young stars of the government. 'He didn't seem to realize that the problem existed but soon became interested when I gave him chapter and verse,' Diana Lamplugh reported. A debate in the House of Commons on the subject was now promised by Hanley, she said.

The main fund-raiser of The Suzy Lamplugh Trust meanwhile was Mary Asprey, who like Mrs Lamplugh threw herself eagerly into the cause. The Lamplughs paid tribute to Mrs Asprey in the *Sunday Express*, where they were quoted as describing her as 'our tower of strength'. Mrs Asprey contributed a report on fund-raising to *The Acorn*, the magazine sent to supporters of the Trust. 'Suzy enjoyed life to the full and we are pleased to say that long faces are not the order of the day at our events,' she wrote. There was a sponsored aerobics exercise event, a bring and buy sale, a school raffle and a sponsored swim at the Unicorn School (Susannah's old school) which raised £5,000. A 'backgammon evening' was held at the Stocks Town and Country Club in King's Road, in which the prizes were a holiday for two in Barbados donated by the tour firm Kuoni, a weekend for two at the Copthorne Hotel given by Prime Communications, and a champagne dinner for four and a year's subscription to Stocks. A special ladies' prize was an antique Wedgwood brooch donated by an antiques business.

A patrons' meeting was held at the House of Lords, and a champagne evening at Phillips Fine Art Auctioneers in which Diana Lamplugh gave a speech and a raffle was drawn by Major-General Sir Jeremy Moore. Susannah's former Face Place client Pamela Spurr-Seager arranged a sponsored swim which was visited by Richard Tracey, then Minister of Sport. 'Easter Monday was a day in Berkeley Square with lunch at Mortons for all the family and an Easter egg hunt,' Mrs Asprey reported in *The Acorn*. 'Everyone also enjoyed an egg and spoon race round the square with a prize for the best decorated egg. Our Patrons' Lunch at the Hotel Inter-Continental was an event which cannot soon be forgotten. The excellent speech made on that occasion by Baroness Young is given in full at the beginning of this newsletter. The food was superb and so was the service.' Another lunch at the Hotel Inter-Continental was planned, as was the Alpha Ball at the Froebel Institute – all in aid of The Suzy Lamplugh Trust. The activities were reported in 'Jennifer's Diary', a social column in *Harper's and Queen*.

The first annual report of the Trust, published 17 months after Susannah went missing, was 24 pages long and highly professionally produced by one of its patrons. The Suzy Lamplugh Trust had long since ceased to be an organization totally overshadowed by the Lamplughs themselves: many others, some of them expert in their fields, had become actively invoved in its work. The first year had shown that many of the Trust's initial assumptions were wrong, the report said. Aggression in the workplace could take many forms, from verbal abuse and misunderstanding to rape – and seven out of ten attacks were on men rather than women. In future the Trust would therefore not just confine its scope to women.

It was also funding a research project at the London School of Economics to examine the extent of aggression at work, and every day it was receiving calls for help from individuals and organizations. A team of speakers, including Diana Lamplugh, was always on hand to visit universities, conferences, companies or any other group that requested it. Relatives of missing people increasingly sought help, often by telephone. Its consultants had provided material for a book by Diana Lamplugh called *Beating Aggression*. And a video, *Avoiding Danger*, showing how both men and women at work could avoid putting themselves unnecessarily at risk, had been made and distributed around the country.

The organization raised more than £100,000 in its first year, it reported, with roughly half coming from fund-raising events and the rest from donations. A quarter then went on direct costs, and 10 per cent as commission to the Trust's fundraiser. Baroness Young, Jeremy Hanley MP, Richard Briers and Mrs Lamplugh herself were among those who contributed to the report. Briers said he was amazed that such a Trust had not been created before. Young said the organization was addressing itself to a previously hidden danger. Baroness Blackstone, the Master of Birkbeck College in London, said she believed the work of the Trust was of great importance.

The chairman of Reed Employment, which helped sponsor the LSE project, said that he had admired the dynamism and organizational flair it had shown. Tim Battle, the Lamplughs' family friend whose idea it had been in the first place, reported a sense of excitement at the realization that The Suzy Lamplugh Trust was beginning to evolve a meaningful role. 'We have made a positive start,' the report concluded. But Battle also pointed out that there was much still to be done and that there was an 'unlimited agenda' ahead.

Throughout this period the publicity continued unabated. Diana Lamplugh developed the theory that her daughter might have been abducted and murdered because she had stumbled upon a mortgage fraud in her work, then refused to go along with it and had been killed as a result. *The Standard* ran the story. 'It's beginning to look more and more like a professional job,' Diana Lamplugh was also quoted as saying in the *Sunday Express*. Because her husband worked for the Law Society and that was the professional body which disciplined recalcitrant lawyers, she reasoned, Susannah might have fallen foul of crooked lawyers who wanted her out of the way. Perhaps they could not afford to include her in. In fact, the detectives had already dismissed the theory. They already knew that some estate agents did indeed regularly receive illegal payments from property developers, but they did not believe that Susannah Lamplugh was in any way involved.

Though Susannah had disappeared many months before,

her mother was as well known as ever to television viewers. 'I was on Channel 4 for a minute last week!' she wrote in one newsletter. 'On Wednesday I was in a programme which was videod for the *Choices* series which go out in June on Sundays for BBC1, I think I may do *Songs of Praise* for them too in July.' Possibly her most celebrated television appearance came when she was a guest on the live national BBC television talk show *Wogan*. Then the substitute host, Sue Lawley, confronted her with the type of difficult question that others apparently felt unable to ask. She knew Mrs Lamplugh must have heard that people were saying she had courted publicity, she said – 'that you have enjoyed, if that's not the wrong word, the limelight'. The programme was nearing its end. This was a terribly cruel thing for them to say, Ms Lawley went on, but how did Diana Lamplugh answer such accusations?

Mrs Lamplugh came back like the television professional she had become. 'Oh, it's funny actually. Lots of people do ask me this. It doesn't occur to me, because I'm doing a job which I particularly know needs doing. I think the thing is that what they underestimate is that when something *horrific* like this happens, you have an *enormous burst of energy* which comes into you. Now that energy has to be used. I wanted to find Suzy. I *terribly* badly wanted to find her. The only way I could use that energy was by actually talking to the press, hoping the press would find her. I mean, I went out to look for her. In looking for her, I got across the police. So that energy is there. It had to be *used*. I found a thing that needed doing. I started the Trust because of that. Now again one had to be very careful. And what I found was that I had to forgive myself. I had to forgive myself for the fact that I couldn't find her. The fact that I couldn't be with her. And the fact that I *enjoy* . . .' Her words trailed off as the *Wogan* signature tune blared out to mark the end of the live show, and the audience erupted into fervent applause.

Chapter Twelve

The disappearance of Susannah Lamplugh was a unique event. It not only led to the biggest missing person inquiry in history, but also became one of the most publicized and celebrated cases of recent times in newspapers, radio and television. This was explained partly by the continuing mystery of what had happened to Susannah, the young woman whom the media persisted in portraying as an uncomplicated person with no problematic areas in her life. The phenomenon of Diana Lamplugh's television appearances and her ready availability for interviews, too, kept police and media interest alive far longer than anyone would have expected.

The passing of a year proved to be a symbolic watershed for all concerned in the case. Three hundred and sixty-five days of intense detective work and media coverage had failed to find Susannah Lamplugh. Newspapers published anniversary features as the time approached, television programmes ran items about the case and Diana Lamplugh gave countless more interviews. Yet hope, somehow, was now in the past. No one involved expected Susannah to return. But for the Lamplughs there was a terrible truth to face as the case moved into its second year: that they might *never* learn either the fate of their daughter or the identity of her presumed abductor. The detectives, too, became increasingly aware that the case would probably never be solved through their efforts.

For the Lamplughs it was a peculiarly harrowing ordeal that had no end. They had never known the finality of seeing a body or a coffin, and it was possible they never would. Yet they had to face a tragic and unexpected loss in the family as much as any other bereaved family. In their case the loss was compounded by the difficulty in mourning or grieving over someone whom they could not totally accept was dead. The parents coped with the uncertainties by throwing themselves energetically into work for The Suzy Lamplugh Trust and by actively monitoring and chivvying the police investigation. Their eldest surviving daughter Tamsin was given some advice by Dr Desmond Kelly, the psychiatrist who was a neighbour of her parents in East Sheen. She *had* to start mourning, he told her, and look back on all the good things about Susannah and their relationship. She should stop 'looking under bushes' for her sister or her assailant and start to get on with her own life.

But the disappearance brought with it unresolved psychological conflict for the family. Though it was illogical to do so, some of them felt guilty over Susannah's disappearance. If only she had not been in New Zealand, Tamsin told herself, she might have been sufficiently close to rescue her sister. Perhaps, in any case, Susannah had wanted to phone her for help the afternoon she went missing, but was unable to do so because Tamsin was not on the phone at home in New Zealand. She knew there was no sense in these feelings, but the inner torment did not end with that awareness. Paul Lamplugh too felt guilty sitting at home when, he thought, he should be out looking for his daughter. His wife felt guilt over the way she had brought up Susannah – to have her freedom, to place so much importance on work, to be ambitious and so on – and feared it all came back to *her*. They both had to forgive themselves for not looking for their daughter all the time either literally or in their minds. They knew the guilt was not logical, but it was very real.

And there was a further underlying internal conflict. It was one terrible paradox that they knew Susannah was no longer alive but could not accept that she was dead; it was another that they had somehow as a family undeniably become more fulfilled in their lives as a result of the tragedy. Both Susannah's sisters and her brother showed more resolve. Tamsin found that she now never held back in life, and always wanted to seize opportunities that presented themselves. The fulfilment was more marked still in the case of Diana Lamplugh. She made no secret of the fact that she enjoyed her television appearances, lectures, and the other work for The Suzy Lamplugh Trust. She greatly relished getting the police, or even the government, to do what she wanted them to do. It was gratifying for her to telephone powerful people and achieve immediate action. Yet all this came about solely because her daughter had disappeared without trace, and that knowledge filled her with guilt. The task for her was to come to terms with it and reconcile one with the other, the satisfaction that arose so unexpectedly from the unbearable.

Another difficulty, keenly felt but hardly articulated by many of those around Paul and Diana Lamplugh, concerned the establishment of The Suzy Lamplugh Trust. The two Lamplugh sisters were not the only ones who had mixed feelings about it. When other relatives heard of the plans, they thought that Susannah's name was being exploited and that there was something wrong – though exactly what was hard to define – about the whole idea. Some of Susannah's friends also felt the same way. But few outsiders felt able to confront the Lamplugh parents with how they really saw the situation. It was only gradually that friends and relatives came to accept the idea. If setting up a Trust that might do some good was the parents' way of dealing with the intolerable burden that had been thrust upon them, they should be free to do so.

Paul and Diana Lamplugh shared another burden. They both doubted inwardly whether Susannah herself would have wanted the establishment of a much-publicized public body in her name (it was only later that Suzy Lamplugh Ventures Ltd was formed). Before her daughter's disappearance Diana Lamplugh had feared that Susannah did not like her. She was afraid that she did not meet her eldest daughter's expectations of what a mother should be. Now, with Susannah's presumed death, she thought that her daughter would want her to be behaving like a conventional mourning parent: wearing black, perhaps passing out with grief, crying. She would certainly not be proud of The Suzy Lamplugh Trust in the way that so many thought she would be; Diana Lamplugh knew – and Paul Lamplugh too thought that his daughter would disapprove of the organization. Yet they were determined that the Trust should exist, to bring good out of evil. It was yet another unanswerable conundrum for them arising out of their daughter's disappearance.

Despite this conflict, Diana Lamplugh's identity – and that of her husband – came to be closely bound up with the Trust. It was as though they could face the awfulness of what had happened to their daughter only by keeping the Trust in her name alive. Two organizations – The Suzy Lamplugh Trust and the British Slimnastics Association – were by now based at the Lamplughs' suburban home, with full-time employees coming to work every day and constant visitors ringing the doorbell. Distinctions between the different worlds soon blurred: one south London social worker who sent for details of Slimnastics was astonished when she also received literature for The Suzy Lamplugh Trust including an appeal for donations. Even Mrs Lamplugh's personal letters to her family were written on the letter-headed notepaper of the Trust. To many she had *become* the Trust, and it helped her to come to terms if not with herself then with the inexplicable mystery of her daughter's disappearance.

Nevertheless it was still hard for all the family to accept that Susannah was gone. Even after the first anniversary of her disappearance Tamsin Lamplugh would read in a newspaper about the latest development in her sister's case, and think to herself for a moment 'I must discuss this with Suze' – before crushingly realizing the truth. Her parents would be caught out when she telephoned them and announced 'Hi – it's me.' The two sisters spoke very similarly, and more than once Paul and Diana Lamplugh thought for a moment that it was Susannah who was finally contacting them. Paul Lamplugh organized a collage of photographs of Susannah, and her presence filled the Lamplugh living room. It could work both ways, though: on one occasion Tamsin Lamplugh pointed out in no uncertain terms to her parents that Susannah had not been the perfect, angelic daughter that she had become after her disappearance.

The events of that summer lunchtime in west London thus changed the lives of so many – not just for the Lamplugh family and close friends like Dave Hodgkinson, but also for policemen and journalists and others who became involved. Diana Lamplugh said that it took some time to realize that people outside the family were also suffering traumas because of what had happened. She would go into her front garden ostensibly to prune the roses, but in reality to give neighbours the opportunity to speak to her; and if she saw people avert their eyes when they saw her coming, she would deliberately go up to them to make it easier for them. Tamsin Lamplugh lost not only her older sister but also her closest friend and confidante. Someone close to the Lamplughs felt that she was the member of the family most devastated by it all, coping not just with the loss but also with the unusual publicity surrounding her mother. She and Susannah's friends pulled together in their grief: well after the first anniversary of Susannah's disappearance she would still go to see Hodgkinson, cling to him, and cry.

Though Diana Lamplugh came to face the likelihood that her daughter was dead, she did not like to consider how she had died. She felt that Susannah would probably have panicked while she was being abducted, and found the experience especially awful; she would have 'frozen' with terror, she feared. Rumours developed throughout Britain that Susannah had gone off deliberately on her own without realizing the impact her disappearance would have – and, seeing all the unexpected publicity, then felt unable to return. Her mother totally discounted that possibility. Even if Susannah could do that to her, she thought, there was no way she could voluntarily cause so much pain to her sisters and brother and father, and her friends. Family friends who thought Susannah might have deliberately gone missing gradually changed their minds as well.

The detectives, too, all but ruled that out as a possibility. There was absolutely no indication that Susannah was planning any kind of disappearance. She had left a half-completed dress on the sewing machine in her flat. She had made plans to collect her missing cheque book on the Monday evening and to go to a party the following night. Her flat was still unsold, and she had not therefore waited for the £70,000 or so (less her outstanding mortgage debt) she could have expected from the sale. She left her office that Monday lunchtime without her lipstick or a comb. She was behaving completely normally. None of this suggested a premeditated disappearance, and those who knew her well believed she simply did not have the ruthlessness to betray so many close to her. Her known friends and contacts were all investigated and none of them, clearly, was shielding her. She was almost certainly not involved in drugs, prostitution or any other kind of crime. It was always possible she had suffered some kind of loss of memory, but with all the intense publicity surrounding the case it was inconceivable that she would not have been recognized sooner or later.

So for the police there was what they called a 'preponderance of possibilities' that Susannah Lamplugh had been abducted and murdered. But how? They thought it likely that after she was last seen by her Sturgis colleagues that Monday lunchtime, she did indeed drive away from Whittingstall Road in her office white Ford Fiesta. She may well have had a genuine appointment with a client, though there remained the possibility that she was meeting someone else – conceivably a man in the property business with whom she was secretly buying a house – and intending to look at 37 Shorrolds Road as a prospective buyer rather than an estate agent. She *probably* then drove the half mile to Shorrolds Road, although it was possible that for some unknown reason she instead headed straight for Stevenage Road, more than a mile in the opposite direction. The detectives remained satisfied that her car was permanently parked in Stevenage Road at least ten minutes before one o'clock on the day she went missing, even though she was also positively sighted more than a mile away in Shorrolds Road at around one o'clock.

The man who succeeded Carter as the senior detective in charge of the case, Detective Superintendent Malcolm Hackett, was succinct when asked what he thought was the solution to the case: 'I do not know what happened to Suzy Lamplugh,' he said simply, and honestly. Every detective working on the case had his or her favourite theory, however, though none could explain away all the conflicting information. But the most favoured theory went as follows, based on instinct as much as hard fact: Susannah could have made her 12.45 appointment on the Saturday morning before her disappearance while she was working a weekend shift in the Sturgis office. A client came in, and they had a few minutes' banter. Lightheartedly, she wrote the name 'Mr Kipper' in her diary, perhaps unclear herself whether the man was being serious or not. The following Monday lunchtime she drove to Shorrolds Road, met the man, and speedily and routinely showed him the house.

Here the theory runs into its first serious conflict. This can have been true only if Riglin and the others who apparently spotted her were each at least a quarter of an hour out in their recollections. But that was possible, especially as some of the witnesses came forward only after a public appeal. So the theory continued. Outside the Shorrolds Road house, 'Mr Kipper' then used some ruse to get Susannah to take him to Stevenage Road. He may have invited her for lunch or a drink – or simply asked to see another Sturgis house for sale in the road. He told Susannah he did not have his car with him in Shorrolds Road, so asked her for a lift. That seemed completely reasonable and with no reason to suspect him – for he was very plausible, and it was a completely humdrum Monday working lunchtime – she readily agreed. He offered to drive her car, doubtless putting forward some seemingly valid reason for doing so. He adjusted the driving seat to fit his longer legs.

Then he suddenly changed character and began to show signs of being the psychopath he actually was. Inside the car for the five-minute drive to Stevenage Road, he pushed his left hand around Susannah's back and locked her door. She now realized something was horribly amiss. Then he pulled up behind his own car beside a garage in Stevenage Road and dragged her out from the passenger's seat through the driver's door – and into his waiting car. She was stricken with fear, he was covering her mouth, and she made no noise. It was all over in less than ten seconds and no one saw what happened. She was still clutching the Sturgis keys to 37 Shorrolds Road and the particulars of the house. He took her in his own car to some unknown place, anywhere in the country. Then he murdered her. In some still undiscovered place he disposed of her body and the keys and house particulars. Before and after all this, on the same day, he talked to people and seemed perfectly normal. No one who meets him routinely ever suspects his secret, that he is a psychopathic killer. He will be apprehended only if he repeats his crime but makes a mistake.

Yet even this theory has numerous flaws in it. It does not explain the discrepancies over the sightings of Susannah in Shorrolds Road and her car in Stevenage Road. It does not explain how Bert Carter and his son Christopher, laying gas pipes in Stevenage Road close to where the car was found, saw and heard nothing. It takes no account of the taxi driver's fare, a man who looked like the flautist James Galway but never came forward, who reported seeing a couple having a 'right ruck' in the street – when the Carters, closer to the scene, saw and heard nothing. It does not explain how Barbara Whitfield, the only one of the witnesses who actually *knew* Susannah, was certain she saw her driving her car with a man beside her in Fulham Palace Road at 2.45 that afternoon. It does not solve the mystery of the telephone calls which Heminsley, the pub landlord who found Susannah's cheque book, insists he received the same afternoon. And it does not explain why there were no clues in Fulham Road, Shorrolds Road or Stevenage Road, or why no body was ever found.

But short of interviewing every single BMW 2000 driver in the country – and if this theory is correct, that connection would be irrelevant because 'Mr Kipper' would probably never have had his car parked in Shorrolds Road – there were no more leads the police could pursue. Having devoted so much time to it, the detectives were none the less reluctant to admit defeat. They had taken more than *six hundred* sworn statements, interviewed *thousands* of people and logged a vast number of telephone calls. But on Day 453 the carousels of index cards were carried personally by Detective Inspector Peter Johnstone and Detective Sergeant Mike Barley, watched by Woman Detective Constable Barbara Harrison, to a storage room in the Hammersmith annexe to which the inquiry had been moved. It was strangely anti-climactic, despite the unspoken emotions and thoughts.

Inwardly the detectives could not help asking where, if anywhere, they had gone wrong. They were satisfied that their investigation had been as thorough as could be, and the Anacapa scrutiny readily confirmed this. Most investigations are won or lost in the first forty-eight hours, and the Lamplugh inquiry was probably no exception. They had been extremely careful to preserve any possible forensic evidence, to launch house-to-house inquiries while the case was still fresh in people's minds, to search all the obvious open spaces and bodies of water. If they had one regret, it was that their subsequent appeal to the public for information centred only on Shorrolds Road and Stevenage Road - as did the *Crimewatch* programme. But by 1.15 that lunchtime 'Mr Kipper' could well have been with Susannah in some other part of London, or even out of the capital altogether. Anyone who thought they had seen Susannah Lamplugh and 'Mr Kipper' outside the narrow confines of Fulham might have felt discouraged from reporting it.

The other controversy, and a subject about which Diana Lamplugh wrote to the Home Secretary to complain – but in the end did not send the letter – was that the investigation was not put on computer. By no means all the detectives were trained to use a computer program in an investigation, and when Susannah Lamplugh first disappeared none dreamed in any case that it would escalate into the type of detailed inquiry that would merit computerization. So they used the time-honoured system of index cards. In essence this is no different from the modern computer system, except that it takes infinitely longer to operate.

Details must be painstakingly entered on the cards and then checked and cross-referenced manually, whereas the police computer system can scan one million words a minute. The system adopted by the Home Office was known as HOLMES, standing for Home Office Major Enquiry System (but with an 'L' added to avoid confusion), but not all the country's police forces used standardized computer language systems. Different police forces could not as a result automatically communicate with others' computers about geographically linked crimes. In the case of the Lamplugh inquiry, the detectives were convinced that even if the case had been put on computer from Day One, the outcome would have been the same – though Mrs Lamplugh felt differently.

However, the Suzy Lamplugh case would not run down quietly. No sooner had the incident room closed than it opened again when detectives became interested in a man arrested for other offences in another part of the country. Diana Lamplugh went on the offensive, telling Deputy Assistant Commissioner

Paul Condon that if there were a police 'cover-up' she would see that questions were asked about the investigation in the House of Commons. ('I was at my most articulate and you would have been proud of me!' she wrote in a subsequent letter to Susannah.) She gave a press conference at the Ritz Hotel (where she was giving a talk on safety at work) but discreetly asked the reporters present not to reveal where she was talking lest it give the wrong impression. She was quoted in *The Independent* as saying that she had had to go and identify bodies. Though this was untrue, she doubtless felt by this time that she *had* been through such experiences.

The man arrested elsewhere was questioned by detectives about Susannah, but was not charged in connection with the case. No evidence was found to link him with her and the police had no alternative but to eliminate him from the case. Neither was any clue obtained as to the whereabouts of Susannah. A medium did promise some vital information and visited Diana Lamplugh in East Sheen Avenue. Then she went into an apparent trance and relived in explicit detail what she said was Susannah's violent end: as ever with the mediums and clairvoyants, the woman's intervention was unhelpful and Mrs Lamplugh was glad to usher her out and receive yet another television crew. Before long the police reclassified the case as still 'Open' – but 'Non-Active'. Everybody familiar with it began to accept the inevitable, that the real story of what had happened on that far-off summer's day might never be known.

Faced with such a frustrating conclusion to this extraordinary case, all those involved had no choice but to get on with their lives. Diana Lamplugh, desperately active with The Suzy Lamplugh Trust, told a magazine that she was 'very impatient' for grandchildren. Paul Lamplugh prepared for a new career outside the Law Society. Tamsin continued to work for the hotel agency and tried to rebuild her life. Elizabeth planned to become the first member of the family to go to university. Richard overcame his dyslexia to the extent that he could study for a degree at a polytechnic. Detective Sergeant Barley studied for his inspector's examinations, and found himself visiting the house of a six-year-old girl to scold her for making a hoax 999 call. Detective Inspector Johnstone settled back to the routine of a CID officer in Fulham, preoccupied with a child rape and one squalid murder and 'suspicious death' after another. Woman Detective Constable Harrison went on a HOLMES computer training course for future investigations.

And Myfanwy, Susannah's faithful family cat, finally died peacefully after a long and cherished life. The cat was one of the last symbolic links between her owner's childhood and her adult independence. Now that link too was gone, and Susannah Jane Lamplugh was not coming back. But she had touched the lives of so many, so unexpectedly.

Postscript

This book started with smiles, and ended in tears. The project began after Diana Lamplugh met Robert McCrum, a Director of the publishers, at a television studio. Soon afterwards she wrote to him to say that she had been besieged by publishers to tell the story of her daughter's disappearance, but wanted to offer it to him first. Following discussions the Lamplughs decided not to write a book themselves, or to use a ghostwriter; they opted to have an independent account, and acknowledged that they could find the result difficult. They went on to negotiate a firm contract with the publishers which gave them a generous advance and royalties. It was vested in their names, but later they announced that their proceeds from the book would go to The Suzy Lamplugh Trust.

Weeks after the contract between the Lamplughs and the publishers had been signed and sealed, I was approached to write the book. By this time Will Sulkin, Editorial Director of the publishers, had taken the project over from McCrum. I duly met the Lamplughs, and agreed to start work almost immediately. It was a very upsetting story and I was frequently affected by it. I talked for hours to Paul and Diana Lamplugh, to members of their family, to Susannah's boyfriends, and to family friends and others. I read through countless family letters that Diana Lamplugh had given me, some of them dating back a decade but others describing in considerable detail the difficult times following Susannah's disappearance. Mrs

Lamplugh was keen that I should talk to the police, and put me in touch with two detectives.

But I sought out other policemen and women at all levels of the Metropolitan Police as well, and received considerable unofficial cooperation from them too. The detectives had not only carefully talked to everyone connected with the tragedy but literally thousands of others too, and in effect I was able to take advantage of their vast research and knowledge of the case. Before long, I knew a great deal about Susannah Lamplugh and her disappearance.

Months later the publishers sent copies of the first six draft chapters to Susannah's parents. The first reaction came from Paul Lamplugh, who told Sulkin how much he liked what he had read and then phoned my home with a similar message. But four days later, he suddenly asked for all the family research material – including Diana Lamplugh's letters – to be returned immediately. He simultaneously wrote to the publishers with a long list of complaints, and also informed them that he and his wife were putting the matter into the hands of solicitors. From that day – before I had written the second half of the book – the Lamplughs cut off all communication with both the publishers and myself. A leading firm of London solicitors acting on their behalf duly wrote to the publishers and to me, repeating the Lamplughs' complaints about the book in strong terms.

Both the publishers and I found ourselves the target of much ire. We then went painstakingly through the Lamplughs' objections, and did so again when they subsequently gave us a similar list for the second half of the book too. In some cases we immediately agreed to what they said; in many more we did not agree but were willing to amend what was written slightly to accommodate their wishes; in the vast majority of cases we felt that in face of the evidence their requests to change or delete passages were simply not justified or reasonable. The publishers then sent them the revised manuscript that incorporated the changes. But by this time Mr and Mrs Lamplugh were seeking to prevent publication of the whole book.

It should therefore go on record that they reject the view of themselves and their daughter in this book. Much of what is written about the family – what they did and how they felt, both before and after Susannah's disappearance – actually came either directly from themselves or their letters, or from other incontrovertible sources. In the case of Susannah's private life, the evidence was equally convincing and was confirmed by the police investigation; but the Lamplughs refused to accept that Susannah had boyfriends other than the ones they knew about.

The dispute over this book lasted months and caused much hurt. My memories of working on it are therefore mixed, but some will always stay with me. I remember, for example, driving across London after first meeting the Lamplughs and listening to a cassette of Susannah's Memorial Service that they had given me. The hymn 'Dear Lord and Father of Mankind', with that peculiarly gentle and unquestioning Anglican pathos, suddenly filled the car: it was all in memory of one Susannah Lamplugh, twenty-five, and I found it deeply moving. Or the feeling of first touching some of Susannah's belongings, her cheque-book stubs and other palpable reminders of a real, vibrant life brought to an inexplicable end. Of a detective dispassionately unlocking a police cabinet and bringing out Susannah's cheque card, diaries, and purse. Or noticing that Paul Lamplugh had set his video machine to record a performance of the *Kindertotenlieder*, Mahler's haunting lament to Rückert's words on the death of children.

And, alas, the memories of lawyers and endless meetings

will also stay with me. Throughout the tribulation over the book, though, the central tragedy of the loss of Susannah Lamplugh's life never diminished for me. There is now a national organization in her memory, and already those affected by similar tragedies have received help and succour from it: her name will thus live on in the minds of so many who never knew her. But for those who did, Susannah Lamplugh was a generous, kind and loving young woman. That is why her loss is so sad, and so outrageous.

Index